DR. PAUL MAJETT ED.D.

Relax! The Machines Will Do It!

Contents

II   Dawn of the digital age (1950s-1970s)

III   Digital Revolution Unfolds (1980s-2020s)

The Boiling Frog and the Cost of Ignorance

The boiling frog effect, although not scientifically precise, demonstrates how a frog could remain in slowly heated water, unaware of the increasing danger, and still be harmed. The metaphor illustrates how people adapt to harmful conditions when changes occur gradually. Instead of reacting to sudden threats, they often overlook slow negative shifts, tolerating worsening situations. Some examples include burnout, unhealthy relationships, and slow responses to climate change, where minor issues accumulate without prompting immediate action. It shows how constant adversity can make harm seem normal, numbing awareness and urgency until the danger turns critical.

Many believe we've become too dependent on technology, particularly Artificial Intelligence, even for simple communication. The erosion of nuanced social interaction is concerning, as individuals lose the ability to interpret subtle body language and vocal tone—skills vital for meaningful, in-person communication. This reliance may also impair face-to-face skills, reduce empathy, lead to misunderstandings, and increase social isolation, despite its convenience.

One big downside of the digital shift is how hard it's become to build genuine empathy. Communicating through screens makes it more challenging to pick up on and understand other people's emotions. Over time, this distance can chip away at our ability to form strong bonds, hurting our real-life relationships. Spending more time in virtual spaces might also dull our emotional awareness and make genuine interactions harder.

The Bureau of Labor Statistics warns that even moderate AI adoption will strain current workforce pipelines, especially in crowded regions. Addressing the shortfall will require more local training and immigration options. By 2030, the U.S. may need 140,000 more skilled trade workers to support AI-driven infrastructure growth.

In 2025, the U.S. government reduced student loan eligibility for degrees no longer considered professional. Faced with these challenges, many young people are choosing alternative paths to achieve economic success. A growing number of Gen Zs are selecting vocational training over a traditional four-year college degree. This route helps them avoid large student debt while building rewarding careers centered on practical skills. It reflects a rising preference for faster, more hands-on ways to attain financial stability and personal fulfillment, with opportunities aligned with their passions and talents.

Despite the challenges it presents, AI offers incredible benefits, such as personalized medicine that could save millions of lives or optimizing supply chains to reduce global waste and improve efficiency. These are powerful goals of progress that humanity is actively pursuing. These benefits, however, come with high hidden costs that society must actively address. The drive for efficiency through automation can gradually diminish human autonomy in decision-making, as algorithms start to make choices for us rather than just helping us.

How did we end up here? We need to look back to understand that. As philosopher George Santayana said, understanding history means learning from past mistakes so we can make better choices now and avoid repeating them. But human nature often gets in the way, so using critical thinking and applying those lessons is key to real progress.

Major technological shifts are seldom passive; they are typically active efforts motivated by humanity's declared, often idealistic, goals of progress, prosperity, and connection. The conflicts and accountability concerns that emerge usually stem from these strong, active ambitions clashing with reality or conflicting social values.

The declared goal of the Machine Age was ambitious: to free humanity from physical labor and scarcity through radical efficiency and mass production, aiming for universal prosperity and an improved quality of life. In contrast, the main aims of the Digital Revolution were connectivity, the democratization of information, and the enhancement of human potential through instant access to knowledge.

To better understand this, we must take a 100-year journey with technology, from the mechanical innovations of the 1920s to a future dominated by AI. We must examine how a gradual adaptation has led to an over-reliance that erodes critical skills and human connection. We must also explore how each technological leap reshaped labor, society, and health, forcing us to confront the profound consequences of a fully integrated, automated world.

I

The Machine Age (1920s-1940s)

*Part 1 summarizes the human-machine relationship during a
significant historical era, combining historical events with
analysis to demonstrate how technology influences society. It
includes examples such as Ford's assembly line and Calvin
Coolidge, and examines themes such as empathy, employment,
education, and shifts from the 1920s to the 1940s. The chapters
connect past innovations to future developments, emphasizing
automation, radio, robotics, and computing.*

1

The Rise of the Machines in the 1920s

I n the 1920s, the water was intriguing as society explored what is often called the "Machine Age." Rapid industrial growth and new technologies have transformed society and culture, changing how people connect with machines. Many hoped mechanizations would spare them exhausting labor, but others feared it would erode human qualities. The 1920s brought both excitement and anxiety. Millions moved from farms to factories.

By the mid-1920s, over ten million Americans worked in mechanical and manufacturing industries, demonstrating America's industrial growth. Yet, this shift also raised concerns about the decline of skilled craftsmanship. Henry Ford's assembly line increased production but turned complex work into repetitive tasks, sparking worries that useful technology might also diminish creativity and human connection.

New Professions in a Mechanized World

In the 1920s, automation advanced with mechanical innovations and electrification. Today, it involves sophisticated interconnected systems that perform complex tasks, analyze data, and make autonomous decisions. Ford improved the assembly line by replacing steam-powered motors with electric ones, boosting efficiency.

Early control systems were simple, using relay logic and basic on-off controls, with human operators monitoring charts and adjusting valves and switches from centralized control rooms. Mechanization involves replacing physical tasks with machines but still depends on human oversight. The breakthrough at that time was Ford's perfect assembly line, as factories shifted from steam power and complex belt systems to electric motors, increasing efficiency and productivity.

As electricity became widespread, homes adopted refrigerators, vacuum cleaners, and washing machines, making chores easier but still requiring some effort. Telephone systems shifted from manual switchboards to automated mechanical setups, changing some tasks while providing only basic, single-purpose automation.

Here, we see automation managing both physical and specific mental tasks by following predefined rules without human intervention. Technological advancements created new jobs for clerical workers operating complex machines, including mechanical and electrical engineers, technicians, and industrial managers. Clerical work expanded with the use of typewriters and early computers.

In 1925, education was strict and teacher-focused, with limited resources. It emphasized classical subjects like Latin and Greek, as well as practical skills such as home economics for girls. Education was rare. Healthcare was improving but still in early stages; doctors still made house calls, hospitals were small, and surgeries were risky due to limited anesthesia and the lack of antibiotics.

Life Between Innovation and Tradition

Around this time, Dr. Rolla Harger developed a scientific method to measure alcohol intoxication, aiming to reduce the dangers of drunk driving. This breakthrough was part of a larger movement to use technology to tackle societal issues and improve public safety.

The electric car starter revolutionized driving by removing the need for hand-cranking, making cars easier to operate. As radios became everyday household items, they increased interest in car ownership and influenced the future of transportation. These innovations made life simpler and addressed ongoing problems. By 1925, fire safety was much less advanced than it is today.

Early fire departments used basic water pumps, and prevention efforts focused on ventilation, fireguards, and asbestos covers, since open flames were still common in homes and businesses. Initial safety measures included electric fire alarms and the first automatic sprinklers, though adoption was slow. Authorities advised people to keep sand or water nearby to extinguish small fires. These basic steps laid the groundwork for future technological progress, improved sanitation, reliable electricity, and broader safety practices.

In 1925, sewage and electricity infrastructure were undergoing a transition. The development of centralized sewage treatment plants, improved sanitation, and a reliable electricity supply marked significant progress. Energy sources shifted from gas lighting and steam power to electricity and fossil fuels, driven by increased use of electric pumps and commercial oil wells.

During this period, the middle class balanced appearances with daily struggles. They enjoyed modern conveniences like gas and electric lighting and indoor plumbing. Over the next hundred years, centralized waste treatment and renewable energy sources would become standard, improving public health and environmental sustainability. For entertainment, they might play the piano or listen to popular radio.

The journey improved, even if limitations remained. Middle-class families could travel farther by train or ship, broadening their experiences beyond their hometowns. In their kitchens, they combined traditional cooking with a few basic labor-saving tools, since pre-packaged foods weren't available yet. People valued personal service and often repaired items rather than replacing them.

The Birth of Modern Technology

Technology had become integrated into daily life and business by the late 1920s. Although online shopping was still far off, early calculating machines and improved cash registers enhanced retail operations. People grew fascinated by machines capable of performing complex tasks, hinting at the potential of AI. Inventions such as the "traffic robot" and the "automatic totalizator" demonstrated early advances in logic and automation. Though simple, these innovations laid the groundwork for the information age.

Other breakthroughs included the first electric hearing aids and the iron lung, which improved the lives of people with respiratory issues. Life in 1925 may have been simpler, but it encouraged innovation that laid the groundwork for modern living.

In the late 1920s and early 1930s, companies like General Motors advanced the automotive industry, while X-rays became widespread, transforming medical diagnostics. These developments, though basic, paved the way for future inventions. Wireless radios delivered news and entertainment into homes and became more affordable. This period also marked the early days of television, which remained out of reach for most until later innovations made it accessible to a broader audience.

Automating telephone exchanges was one of the earliest glimpses of artificial intelligence, making communication more efficient and reducing the need for human operators. These antique machines marked a significant step forward in long-distance communication, which at the time relied on the postal service.

Workers in Transition

As traditional roles developed, the pace of change sped up. With AT&T's expansion, applications have become increasingly important. Before automation became widespread, demand shifted toward operators and inspectors, who required technical skills and thus became more valuable. Demand grew for technicians and engineers capable of connecting innovation with practical use, leading to greater specialization in tasks.

Concerns about dehumanization persisted, driven by the repetitive, fragmented nature of the work. Even as more jobs appeared, doubts remained about job quality and how mechanization affected worker motivation and satisfaction in farming. The Machine Age brought exciting progress but also left a lingering sense of unease.

Census and labor records show a shift from farming to manufacturing and services. Work has become more efficient with machines taking on heavy tasks, allowing roles to focus more on skills, creativity, and intellect rather than on losing jobs. Data indicate better working conditions, higher education needs, and more women participating in the workforce, reflecting broader opportunities.

Despite these advancements, concerns about job losses increased. Introducing scientific management into tourism improved efficiency but also threatened the job security of assembly line and foundry workers. This environment encouraged the development of industrial psychology, with figures such as Hugo Münsterberg examining how mechanization affected workers' mental health. They introduced measures to improve hiring, training, and workplace conditions, balancing employer goals with employee well-being.

Human factors in engineering focus on theories that better align technology with human abilities. Multidisciplinary teams examined how people interact with machines to reduce errors and mental fatigue. The goal was to ensure that technological progress supports rather than overrides core human values.

Concerns about the loss of autonomy became a focus of critiques of mechanization. Many workers believed these tools diminished their skills, sparking debate over the effects on individuals and the community. As automated processes expanded, they also introduced new vulnerabilities, prompting people to think more carefully about the broader impact of relying on technology.

In union halls and everyday conversations, the focus shifted from pay and working conditions to larger concerns about becoming obsolete and losing personal control. The daily grind of factory life influenced how people viewed their free time and relationships, changing both through the lens of impersonal technology.

In 1925, key figures like President Calvin Coolidge, Vice President Charles G. Dawes, and Secretary of Commerce Herbert Hoover played influential roles in U.S. politics during an exciting era. Major banks such as J.P. Morgan & Co., National City Bank of New York, and Chase National Bank contributed to the growth of the modern economy. The Roaring Twenties ended with the onset of the Great Depression.

The shift from a vibrant, innovative era to the harsh realities of the 1930s marked a significant change. Radio, once just for fun and entertainment, became an essential means of sharing important news during difficult economic times. Industries that depended on consumer spending, such as car manufacturing, faced significant challenges staying afloat.

By the late 1920s, economic hardship threatened the US. Although the Roaring Twenties brought excitement, they also caused increasing economic concerns. The telephone, supported by AT&T's expanding network, accelerated communication and laid the foundation for future data-sharing innovations. The influence of the internal combustion engine extended well beyond automobiles, revolutionizing farming and industry while enhancing efficiency.

Innovations marked a major technological shift, leading to the disappearance of older technologies from daily life and their replacement by broadcasts discussing economic issues. The financial limitations of that period challenged the potential of automation and early artificial intelligence, shaping the future direction of technological development.

The Rise of Intelligent Automation

These days, automation relies on artificial intelligence and constant connectivity to perform tasks with minimal human input across various industries. Modern factories utilize robotic arms, CNC machines, and integrated systems. Innovations such as digital twins and IoT enable real-time monitoring, automated adjustments, and data-driven decisions.

Back in the 1920s, cars always required a human at the wheel, but today's vehicles include features like self-parking and adaptive cruise control, moving toward full autonomy. The significant change is in the extent to which modern technology has advanced and become adaptable. While past machines handled simple tasks, today's AI and machine learning systems handle much more complex societal tasks.

Modern automation advances even further, with intelligent systems making tough decisions and performing physical work, transforming society's operations. Infrastructure planning and public safety considerations played a pivotal role in the transition to personal transportation. The U.S. government did not initially fund automobile development; instead, it funded the massive road infrastructure required for adoption. The Federal Aid Road Act of 1916 and subsequent acts spurred the construction of nationwide highway systems, making long-distance automobile travel feasible and necessary.

By the 1930s, technology was becoming important in daily life, with ancient ideas in computing and robotics taking shape. The Great Depression raised concerns about job security and social changes. Analyzing this period with historical data and a modern perspective reveals how people adapted and persevered amid rapid change. They balanced innovation with the protection of human values as progress moved forward.

The Dawn of the Great Depression

During the Great Depression, families relied on entertainment radio as a vital source of distraction and connection. As broadcasting expanded and programs grew more engaging, it provided a much-needed respite from everyday struggles. Its flexibility highlighted how technology could shape the public mood and unite people. Although the term 'AI' wasn't used, the early developments laid the groundwork for automation and increased connectivity. This era implied that machines would eventually play a crucial role in everyday life.

Groups leading discussions at the time frequently shared early insights into employment, wages, and workplace conditions. The reports indicated increased productivity, economic growth, and social change. While there was optimism about improved job prospects, concerns remained about the potential for machines to replace human roles.

Manufacturing had become the primary focus, drawing much attention. Despite its dangers, mining still employed over a million people. Advances in mechanization lowered the need for farm labor, while the thriving automobile industry represented modern progress, creating hundreds of thousands of new jobs.

2

The Human Response to Machines in the 1930s

D uring the 1930s, families faced significant challenges because of the Great Depression and relied on ingenuity and careful spending. While innovative technologies were emerging, most households lacked the means to access them, so their lives were a mix of old-fashioned hard work and aspirations for progress.

In the 1930s, humans and machines worked together, with people controlling, setting goals, and supervising the process. Machines handled physical labor or simple calculations, but the idea of autonomous, intelligent machines was still a concept in fiction and academic debates. Unlike today's seamless collaboration, people back then had to adapt to the limitations of machines, often relying on tools like punch cards and complex interfaces.

Unemployment was a primary concern throughout the decade, influencing how people perceived the link between society and technology. In the 1930s, the Great Depression worsened already troubling labor statistics. By 1933, about 15 million Americans—one in four workers—were unemployed. The industrial slowdown, combined with fears that machines were replacing human workers, fueled this rise in unemployment. Once celebrated for promoting progress and efficiency, machines came to symbolize human displacement, increasing worries about the future of work and society.

Even during economic hardships and some uncertainty about new technologies, the 1930s saw growth in employment sectors, although losses still outweighed gains. As machines became more advanced, the demand for specialists, such as mechanics and technicians, grew. These skilled workers kept everything from textile looms to early accounting machines running smoothly.

Working with early computers demands sharp logic and attention to detail. These specialized roles, often found in large companies or emerging research labs, marked the rise of a new workforce. However, for many who had lost jobs in traditional industries, these opportunities remained out of reach because their skills did not match those used on farms or factory floors. The result was a more divided job market and growing unease, as many workers faced fewer promising job prospects and limited access to retraining.

Relying on technology forced people to adapt their thinking to fit the rigid frameworks machines required. Using punch card systems and managing complex mechanical controls became part of daily life, a stark contrast to the intuitive digital tools we have today. Thinking machines then remained fiction, not reality.

The Birth of Automation in the 1930s

The period marked the rise of early mechanical and electrical control systems designed for specific, rule-based tasks in factories and homes. Most of these systems used simple "on-off" switches and basic temperature controls, with new components like micro-switches and precise electrical timers appearing for the first time. Some experimental automated plants, such as the A. O. Smith Corporation's auto frame manufacturing plant, showed progress but focused more on mechanization than real automation. This shift replaced physical strength and manual labor with machines.

By 1930, electricity illuminated 70% of U.S. homes, boosting the popularity of appliances like refrigerators, washing machines, and vacuum cleaners. In factories, electric motors replaced steam engines, improving efficiency and productivity. Early industrial controls, consisting of simple switches and controllers, began to develop, though most systems still required manual operation. The focus was on simplifying processes, paving the way for future automation advances.

Radio and Resilience in the Great Depression

The Great Depression affected daily life and slowed technological progress during the 1930s. The Roaring Twenties' lively energy gave way to widespread hardship, with breadlines and soup kitchens becoming familiar sights. Families turned to radios for both comfort and guidance as broadcasts shared the harsh realities of stock market crashes and high unemployment. Still, the radio remained a household essential, providing news, entertainment, and a much-needed sense of community.

Radio was a key source of news and entertainment, bringing families together to hear updates on economic recovery and daily happenings. Even when other technological progress slowed, radio continued to evolve, with improved vacuum tube designs enhancing sound quality. It became even more critical as it provided both an escape and valuable information, helping families get through tough times. Other inventions, such as the telephone, became essential tools for those who could afford them, helping maintain business and personal connections.

During the Depression, radios became an essential gadget, providing families with a crucial mix of entertainment and news. Advances in vacuum tube technology and broadcasting improved sound quality, making radio a daily necessity. Stations offered listeners news, dramas, and comedy shows, providing a welcome break from tough economic times. Radio stations exposed audiences to a wide range of artists and genres, boosting record sales and shaping popular music culture. The emergence of electric instruments like guitars and keyboards created new creative avenues for musicians and songwriters.

Between 1925 and 1930, the entertainment industry experienced a significant transformation. Movie theaters became an affordable escape for the public, and simpler leisure activities gained popularity. Meanwhile, government efforts focused on national security and economic recovery, which prompted earlier research into packet switching and data networks. This foundation led to technology booms like the ".com" era, shifting technology from broadcast-only systems to pave the way for the connected world that followed.

Movies offered a welcome escape from everyday struggles; for those who couldn't afford the latest gadgets, card games, board games, and reading became treasured hobbies. Meanwhile, the broadcasting industry focused on delivering a richer listening experience by refining techniques and improving sound quality through technological advancements.

The Great Depression shifted fashion from luxury to practicality, reducing demand for fancy clothing but increasing the popularity of affordable ready-to-wear styles, which helped support jobs in the industry. The period also sparked innovation, with synthetic fabrics providing budget-friendly alternatives to traditional materials. Mass media, like radio and early television, helped spread new trends, influencing consumer tastes and creating alternative career paths in fashion journalism and styling.

Early Robotics and Computing Foundations

During this decade, the earliest industrial robots appeared, with manipulators designed to replicate human joints and perform tasks such as pulling and lifting on factory floors. A memorable highlight was the 1939 World's Fair, where "Elektro," a seven-foot-tall robot, amazed audiences by walking, talking, and carrying out basic tasks. The display captivated the audience, generating both excitement and a touch of concern about the future of technology.

Key breakthroughs in computing occurred during this period. In 1939, Konrad Zuse built one of the first programmable electromechanical computers, using binary logic with electric switches. Thinkers like Alan Turing and Kurt Gödel advanced mathematical logic, laying the groundwork for the concept of artificial intelligence. Human "computers"—often women—played a key role in fields such as aerospace, highlighting the ongoing importance of human intellect in solving complex problems.

The Innovations of the Great Depression

The financial struggles during the Great Depression pushed businesses to find new ways to operate more efficiently and reduce costs, leading to the adoption of automated financial record-keeping. In transportation, the decline in disposable income hurt car sales, but the downturn spurred innovations in the automotive industry.

More affordable models and flexible payment options emerged, demonstrating the industry's resilience and paving the way for recovery. Communication technology advanced as telephones became common, and calculating machines improved, paving the way for easier information sharing.

Even during the Great Depression, innovation thrived, resulting in remarkable inventions like the drunkometer. Invented by Dr. Rolla Harger, this device measured alcohol levels from breath samples, making significant advances in road safety and law enforcement. The electric starter for cars became popular, replacing the laborious hand-cranking process and making car ownership more accessible. These innovations demonstrated resilience and creativity as society embraced technology to improve life during tough times.

The Human Cost of Automation

The 1939 World's Fair, featuring its star attraction Elektro, showcased both optimism for the future and concern about economic difficulties and job loss. In everyday life, the constant hum of new machines in workplaces and public spaces created a sense of hope for progress alongside quiet worries about being replaced.

Technological progress continued to influence culture and ideas, with the radio becoming a crucial source of news and entertainment, providing comfort during tough economic times. However, as daily routines became more mechanized, concerns arose about standardization and the decline of human connection. Machines started to impact not only employment but also thought and interaction.

As machines gained influence beyond the factory floor, they sparked the creation of industrial psychology. People began to see workers as individuals rather than interchangeable parts. Broadcasts and standardized methods shaped a mechanized mindset, fostering both trust in and doubt about technology's growing role.

For many people, machines also brought difficult times. Skilled workers, like machinists, saw their jobs threatened or even lost as mechanical arms and automated systems took over. The decade's major inventions—refrigerators, washing machines, tractors—shared the stage with the sadness of factory shutdowns and the stress of unemployment. Although these advancements made household chores easier and increased work efficiency, they revealed the paradoxical nature of progress.

Talks about early computers and robotics stirred both excitement and unease. Even in their experimental stages, these technologies sparked questions about the future of human roles and what counts as meaningful work. During the Great Depression, society's reliance on machines became a bigger talking point, showing how progress could open doors while also exposing new weaknesses.

In the 1930s, a more balanced and practical outlook developed. A combination of necessity, skepticism, and hesitant admiration for machines characterized the era. People's roles shifted from complete control to careful supervision, as technology could both empower and restrict. Tough times, new inventions, and cultural unease prompted society to reflect, laying the foundation for the growing relationship between humans and machines.

The Evolution of Automation and AI

The concept of artificial intelligence dates to ancient times and has endured challenging economic eras. One notable instance is the "automatic totalizator," a mechanical apparatus constructed in the early 20th century that adjusted betting odds in real time, serving as an early illustration of machine learning.

This electromechanical system, implemented at racetracks, enabled real-time wager recording, dynamic odds calculation, and the display of totals on tote boards. It optimized the pari-mutuel betting process by accurately calculating bets. Its primary role was to manage pool betting by collecting wagers, applying a fee, and distributing winnings. The device securely logged bets from various stations, summed totals for each horse, calculated the total pool, and displayed real-time updates and provisional odds.

It was a mechanical computer built to calculate betting odds at racetracks. Here, AI introduces machine cognition and adaptability. For example, when someone wagers on horses like Lightning, Thunder, and Storm, all these processes happen smoothly. Before automating the totalizator, manual betting was slow and error-prone.

Although simple, these innovations foreshadowed a future in which machines could learn and adapt, paving the way for later advances in AI. Modern automation combines innovative computer technology, data-driven systems, and artificial intelligence that can make complex decisions and learn. Industrial robots perform detailed tasks with accuracy and speed, while AI manages cognitive tasks such as image recognition and data analysis. Thanks to the Internet of Things (IoT), we now have "smart" factories where machines connect, share information, and adapt—often without human input.

Automation has extended well beyond manufacturing into the digital realm, with software now managing everything from customer service to financial modeling. Self-driving cars, autonomous drones, and automated guided vehicles show a level of independence that would have been unthinkable in the 1930s.

The fundamental differences between automation in the 1930s and today are in scope and intelligence. Back then, automation involved fixed, single-purpose machines that needed human intervention for adjustments. Today, it's all about adaptable, programmable, and intelligent systems that can respond to new challenges, learn from data, and manage complex, non-routine tasks across various industries.

3

Human-Machine Relations in the 1940s:
A Transitional Decade

In the 1940s, people's ability to adapt influenced their operation of complex machinery, especially in industrial settings and early computers. Handling these machines requires a detailed understanding of their controls and strong technical skills. As technological advancements accelerated, this relationship evolved, leading to new ways humans would interact with technology in the future.

The main goal of technology in the 1940s was national survival, quickly followed by a focused effort to apply wartime efficiency and innovation to promote widespread domestic prosperity. One of the most important technological breakthroughs of that time was the development of radar using the cavity magnetron. This essential component laid the groundwork for the development of the commercial microwave oven.

A typical 1940s family day centered on chores, community, and resourcefulness, shaped by the impact of World War II and the economic struggles after the Great Depression. Technology primarily reduced physical labor and provided entertainment, though many tasks still required manual effort.

During this decade, the job market changed. Wartime needs fueled a significant increase in industrial output, creating more manufacturing jobs—over 15 million by 1944—showing just how strong the nation's industry had become. Farming still employed many people, but mechanization reduced the number of jobs. People from rural areas had to learn new technical skills to operate factory equipment, such as looms and early calculators. Production shifted, replacing manual labor with technical methods.

Shifting From Manual Labor to Machine Mastery

As the industrial sector grew, new job types emerged. Although the term "automation" wasn't yet standard, its basic ideas were clear in how complex machines were built and maintained. Skilled technicians played a vital role, handling tasks such as fine-tuning precision tools, repairing intricate gear systems, and operating early automated assembly lines in specialized industries.

Early computing, driven by military and scientific needs, involved "computers." These were women who performed complex calculations manually, using mechanical tools. Their work demanded strong math skills and meticulous attention to detail, making them vital to the operation of emerging technological systems.

The Automation Industry in the 1940s

Automation was in its early stages, focused on mechanization and the initial use of automatic control systems for mass production. Although it was not as advanced as today's technologies, it has advanced over the years, leading to significant growth.

In the 1940s, "automation" referred to the automated handling of materials and parts in manufacturing. The drive for greater efficiency and output during wartime sped up this development. At that time, mechanization was the primary form of automation, exemplified by Henry Ford's assembly lines.

Early industrial setups used simple feedback mechanisms, such as the flying-ball governor, in steam engines. Today, industries with high production demands—such as textiles, chemicals, and tobacco—operate through automated systems. Specialized machines perform specific, repetitive tasks with impressive consistency.

Machines in this era were purely mechanical, designed for one purpose and unable to be reprogrammed or repurposed, which made them rigid. As the U.S. moved from the struggles of the 1930s into the global conflicts of the 1940s, technological progress sped up. Innovations from the Depression, especially in radio and early networking, laid the groundwork for rapid advances during the war and the prosperous years afterward.

In 1941, the completion of the Z3 represented a major technological breakthrough as the first operational, programmable, automatic digital computer. Despite its revolutionary nature, the technology was still in its early stages, and industries had yet to adopt or integrate it into automation processes.

The radio, a crucial source of news and entertainment during tough times, remained at the forefront. Its role expanded as it integrated with new visual technologies and with older ideas about digital data transmission. Observing a more connected world emerging, driven by resilience and creativity born from economic hardships.

Big department stores like Sears and Macy's dominated the shopping scene, while five-and-dime stores offered affordable options. RadioShack was a popular electronics retailer that reflected the growing fascination with radios, TVs, and early computers. Police and fire departments upgraded their equipment with two-way radios for quicker communication, and fire crews received powerful pumpers and tall ladder trucks that revolutionized firefighting.

Old sewage and sludge disposal systems posed health risks in minority neighborhoods. While expanded power grids and new plants increased electricity access, rural and minority areas still experienced unreliable service. Schools used typewriters and slide rules, and some advanced classrooms began experimenting with early computers.

The global conflicts of the 1940s accelerated technological progress, laying the foundation for a future that would transform work. Practical skills in operating and repairing complex machinery pointed to the more abstract, system-level thinking required as machines strengthened into semiautonomous tools. Workforce trends indicate millions adapted to the pace of factory work, while a smaller, emerging group began exploring advances in computing and mechanics.

Wealth, Race, and Education in the 1940s

Despite widespread adoption of technology, wealth inequality persisted. Radio became common, but phones remained limited to wealthy households, who also had access to advanced models with international broadcasts. In 1940, white families earned an average of $2,340, while minority families earned $1,216—a gap that restricted resources and quality of life, further worsened by discrimination and segregation.

In 1940, New York was the nation's largest city and a center of culture and commerce, but sharp wealth gaps divided its boroughs. Affluent residents lived in areas like Manhattan's Upper East Side, while the poor endured cramped, overcrowded tenements. Houston, much like Dallas, thrived on booming prosperity, while rural towns in the Dust Bowl region faced poverty and high unemployment.

General Motors, Standard Oil, and U.S. Steel grew into major industrial giants, while financial powerhouses such as J.P. Morgan, Chase National Bank, and Bank of America amassed immense wealth. Prominent families such as the Rockefellers, Vanderbilts, and Astors wielded significant economic and political influence, amassing their fortunes in a society marked by deep segregation.

Income disparities influenced housing access, with white families more likely to own homes while many minority families rented. After the war, suburban growth surged thanks to government loans and the GI Bill, but discriminatory practices and redlining excluded minority communities. These neighborhoods fostered resilience and a strong cultural identity through mutual support.

Marriner Eccles, the Federal Reserve chairperson, played a significant role in shaping the financial landscape of the 1940s. His monetary policies helped stabilize the economy and laid the groundwork for post-war prosperity.

Known for his expertise and steady leadership during tough times, Eccles became a prominent figure in economics.

Franklin D. Roosevelt led the United States through the war years, with his New Deal policies fueling economic recovery and social progress. Meanwhile, across the Atlantic, Winston Churchill inspired resilience in the United Kingdom. Roosevelt's grasp of financial issues and his skill in guiding the nation during difficult times earned him a reputation as a keen economic strategist.

World War II changed household structure and size. With many men absent because of war, women took on roles in earning money and raising children, filling jobs previously held by men. Families often grew smaller as people moved for jobs or to contribute to the war effort.

World War II sparked rapid advances in technology, especially in code-breaking and computing, with groundbreaking machines such as Colossus and ENIAC paving the way for future developments. When the war ended, it ushered in a new era where progress in artificial intelligence and computer automation continued to transform society.

In the 1940s, white and minority families faced notable disparities in income and opportunity, seen in unequal education and technology access. While schools emphasized vocational skills, minority institutions often lacked the resources to support such programs. Nonetheless, communities united through social networks and self-help efforts, fostering resilience and a shared sense of purpose.

With higher incomes, many white families could afford cars and travel, luxuries that were often out of reach for minority families. Sparse public transportation made it harder for minority neighbors to access jobs and resources. Women gained new independence through work, though returning veterans sometimes forced them back into traditional roles. Leisure travel increased for those with the means, but discrimination and financial obstacles continued to limit opportunities for minority families.

Technological advancements opened new opportunities across various sectors. Women who demonstrated their skills during the war shifted into fields like computing and engineering. This effort played a key role in reducing gender gaps and encouraging greater inclusion in society.

During this decade, technology increasingly influenced education, but access varied among schools. While typewriters and slide rules were standard in classrooms, some institutions also introduced early computers. Film projectors and radio broadcasts offered glimpses of the broader world, delivering educational programs that fostered unity and a shared experience among students.

The idea of the "robot" became popular in culture, often shown as artificial beings made to serve humans, but sometimes depicted as menacing. This theme captured both fascination and unease about mechanical beings and their role in society.

Technology, Warfare, and Society in the 1940s

World War II in the 1940s spurred rapid progress in aviation, radar, cryptography, and medicine. Machines served both as tools of destruction and lifesaving devices. The atomic bomb showcased the frightening power of technological progress. On the home front, wartime production and rationing emphasized the vital role of technology in everyday life.

Electricity became widespread, making home appliances common despite wartime shortages. By the end of the decade, early electronic computers appeared for military and scientific purposes. This period saw increased reliance on technology, raising ethical concerns about its effects.

Jet engines and commercial aviation, along with the atomic bomb, demonstrated the power of technology. The rise of electronic computers in the 1940s marked the start of the digital era and revolutionized data processing. Inventing the transistor in 1947 opened the door to smaller, more efficient electronic devices. These breakthroughs shaped the post-war world and laid the foundation for future technological advancements.

In advanced classrooms, early computers such as the Mark I and ENIAC debuted, though access was not widespread. Minority schools often missed out on these innovations, while film projectors and radio broadcasts provided new ways for students to connect with the broader world. Powerful machines like ENIAC sped up data processing, leaving a significant mark on science, engineering, commerce, industry, and government.

Organizations adopted computers to increase efficiency and foster innovation, with businesses streamlining inventory management and financial institutions enhancing economic analysis. Governments also employed computers to handle population data and improve military strategies.

The creation of crash test dummies revolutionized automotive safety by streamlining the development of safety features and fostering a safety-first mindset, which in turn spurred further innovation. Around that time, George de Mestral invented Velcro, a clever yet simple invention whose versatility led to uses in clothing, footwear, the automotive industry, and even the aerospace industry.

Factories adopted machines for automation, taking on dangerous, repetitive, or exhausting tasks to uphold the legacy of the Industrial Revolution. This shift allowed workers to move from hard labor to roles that require technical knowledge and smart oversight. The focus shifted from just physical effort to innovation and guidance, creating space for creativity and more engaging work.

The Conceptual Foundations of AI

The emergence of abstract computer mathematics has prompted discussions among scholars and scientists regarding the capabilities of thinking machines. This branch of mathematics underpins many everyday technologies, often working behind the scenes. Typical instances include cryptography and data management. For example, digital signatures rely on abstract mathematical concepts to authenticate software updates, emails, and online documents. They help ensure data integrity and prevent senders from denying their messages (non-repudiation).

The concept of artificial intelligence (AI) shifted from science fiction to serious research. Engineers envisioned machines capable of learning and solving problems beyond their initial programming. This early enthusiasm for conceptual thinking generated a shared curiosity that appeared in academic journals and scientific conferences. The goal was for machines to work alongside humans, extending our intellectual capabilities.

An increasing reliance on technology shaped the decade. Outside factories, families turned to radios with complex vacuum tubes for news and connection. Electricity powered daily comforts and essentials, while typewriters allowed long-distance communication. Skills with mechanical processes were crucial in many fields, from pilots in cockpits to cryptographers cracking codes. Throughout it all, humans remained the driving force behind the machines, whether for good or bad.

By the end of the decade, electronic computers had emerged, operating on abstract math and logical gates. They required not just skill but also a deep understanding of their inner workings. Scientists and engineers moved from merely operating them to designing the future, in which machines might begin to mimic human thought. The idea of intelligent machines was no longer just science fiction—it was becoming a serious area of study.

The rise of intelligent machines is raising the possibility of job losses in roles involving repetitive analytical tasks. In the 1940s, AI hadn't yet led to widespread unemployment, but the concepts shaping its future were already developing. Before electronic devices, "computers" referred to people performing calculations manually. As farming and manufacturing became more mechanized, many jobs evolved.

The U.S. Bureau of Labor Statistics offers detailed employment trend data from that era. Concise reports and compact yearbooks highlight the labor shifts as agriculture became more mechanized and manufacturing processes more efficient, reducing the need for manual labor. Emerging advanced computing machines foreshadowed the automation of complex calculations and data processing, a trend well documented in historical records.

Rise of Intelligent Systems

In the late 1940s, wartime technological advances carried over into peacetime, leading to significant breakthroughs. The transistor enabled smaller electronics and paved the way for personal computing. While many innovations remained specialized, digitalization had begun transforming information management.

Wartime progress in computing and automation found new uses that boosted efficiency and opened new opportunities. Throughout the decade, science and engineering became part of everyday life, building confidence in technology's potential to create a better future. Automation has expanded into a connected digital world where machines handle complex tasks.

Modern robots utilize advanced sensors for precise assembly, welding, and inspection. With AI, these systems can learn, adapt, and make instant decisions—an essential advancement from what was possible in the 1940s. IoT links everything, making factory equipment smarter through predictive maintenance, efficient inventory management, and remote monitoring.

RPA and similar tools continue to transform industries by automating administrative tasks and reshaping workplaces and manufacturing processes. Automation now influences everyday life, from self-driving cars and self-checkout stations to smart home devices and efficient logistics. Software-based systems offer greater flexibility, enabling easy reprogramming to meet new requirements. What began as simple mechanical aids has developed into intelligent systems capable of managing a broad spectrum of cognitive and physical tasks.

The 1940s marked a significant shift in how humans interacted with machines, as wartime demands accelerated technological progress. People quickly adapted to complex devices, new specialized roles appeared, and dependence on machines grew. This decade set the stage for modern computing and showed how technology can transform work and society.

II

Dawn of the digital age (1950s-1970s)

Part 2 outlines the development of human-machine relationships from the 1950s to the 1970s, emphasizing key technological, social, and economic shifts. The transistor, automation, and freeway expansion demonstrate both benefits and challenges, such as job losses and increased inequality. This section highlights significant technological progress and its effect on society.

4

Interactions Between Humans and Machines During the 1950s

During the 1950s, suburban neighborhoods expanded, families experienced a strong sense of community, and household gadgets and new forms of entertainment became increasingly common. While family roles were usually well-defined, technological advances began to change daily routines, making some chores easier and introducing new social interactions.

By the 1950s, the water in the pot had reached a comfortable temperature. Workers were now using technology to boost their physical abilities, thereby transforming the relationship between people and machines. Early computers, impressive for their time, were giant calculators that depended on human guidance. These machines weren't autonomous, and this relationship shaped how technology became part of industry and science during that period.

After World War II, demand for new appliances increased rapidly as Americans aimed to modernize their homes for greater comfort and efficiency. Consumers viewed these technologies as investments that saved time and effort, helping to achieve an ideal American lifestyle. The idea of "better living through electricity" motivated families, especially homemakers, to choose products that offered convenience and stability.

The 1950s not only had practical applications but also sparked discussions and research that laid the groundwork for AI development. Mathematicians and engineers began questioning whether machines could show intelligence, learn, and solve problems. These initial ideas went beyond treating machines as mere calculators, envisioning a future in which they collaborate with humans on creative and intellectual tasks. This era marked a pivotal turning point, with pioneering ideas overshadowing current human-machine interactions and guiding future directions.

Before that era, jobs were mainly in industry and agriculture. Manufacturing grew due to post-war demand, providing many jobs, while farming declined but remained significant. Early automation began changing workplaces as assembly lines adopted increasingly automated systems. This shift increased the demand for skilled workers to operate, maintain, and design machinery. New positions, such as electromechanical technicians and machine operators, emerged, highlighting a future in which technological skills would be crucial.

During the 1950s, automation primarily targeted mechanical tasks. Industrial robots and the earliest computers replaced repetitive work in factories and office calculations. As a result of these advances, traditional jobs such as bookkeeping and typing decreased, while new opportunities in information technology and data processing emerged.

Automation now integrates AI, robotics, and task-optimization software. This evolution moves beyond simple automation to advanced systems that fundamentally change industries and roles. In 1950, the U.S. experienced swift social and economic shifts. Post-World War II, a wave of technological innovation emerged, marked by the introduction of the transistor. This tiny yet influential device aimed to revolutionize everyday life and work by offering enhanced convenience and accessibility.

For middle-class families, the 1950s represented a blend of tradition and change. They experienced color television, the rise of rock and roll, and a surge in car ownership. However, many daily habits and values still echoed the past. Transistors transformed household electronics, replacing bulky vacuum tubes and paving the way for improvements in hearing aids and early computers.

The transistor's influence reached far beyond consumer electronics, triggering a significant transformation in the American economy. It fueled competition as companies sought to integrate transistors into existing products and develop new ones. At the same time, the flight data recorder, known as the black box, was designed to log both flight data and cockpit communications. This innovation boosted aviation safety and prompted discussions about privacy and data rights. These 1950s advancements cemented the US's position as a global leader in innovation, enhancing daily life and influencing future developments.

The Birth of Technical Roles in the Age of AI

In the 1950s, early AI theory, though still abstract, suggested the emergence of new job opportunities. As research advanced into logic, learning, and machine problem-solving, roles in programming, systems analysis, and AI research began to develop. These positions demanded both technical skill and conceptual insight, moving away from manual, repetitive work that had long been prevalent. This period signaled the beginning of a transition toward careers focused on creating, managing, and understanding intelligent systems, laying the foundation for the modern technological era.

In the 1950s, machines supported physical tasks, while humans handled decision-making and work management. At NASA, teams of human "computers"—mainly women with strong math skills—performed complex calculations. Over time, electronic computers such as ENIAC and UNIVAC replaced manual calculations. Although not intelligent, these computers were powerful tools that eased the workload, but they still required human operation and interpretation of outputs.

Exploring Social Class Divides in 1950s America

As technology progressed, the gap between social classes became clear. Wealthy families maintained a higher standard of living than many in the middle and lower classes could achieve. Initially, transistor radios were luxury items reserved for the rich, but over time, they became affordable for the average household.

The discrepancy was most noticeable in transportation, where cars became a symbol of status and freedom. Wealthy families drove luxurious vehicles, while those with fewer resources relied on public transit or older modes of transportation such as horse-drawn carriages. Although unequal, the 1950s were hopeful times, with the transistor era opening new opportunities, even if not everyone benefited.

The transistor age, although seen as a luxury, sparked optimism and a sense of possibility across all social classes. While the wealthy enjoyed innovations like sleek transistor radios and advanced cars, the middle class also aspired to own them. Over time, the benefits of technological progress became more accessible, fueling dreams of upward mobility.

Automobiles continued to symbolize privilege, with wealth leading the transportation revolution. Yet as the decade progressed, more families acquired cars and adopted the expanding culture of mobility and advancement, reducing the social gap.

The Story of America's Freeway Revolution

Expanding the freeway network in the 1950s transformed the American landscape. Better roads connected remote towns, sparking businesses such as motels and gas stations that later became convenience stores. The automotive industry boomed, with Detroit at its core, and car dealerships and repair shops thrived.

The growth of automobiles and highways caused a decline in industries reliant on rail transport. As road travel became more convenient, fewer passengers used trains, leading to a deterioration in train station activity. Despite these changes, the period remained characterized by progress and optimism.

The development of the freeway system not only altered the physical landscape but also triggered technological and business innovations that influenced American society. During the 1950s, significant changes and challenges emerged, impacting communities such as Black Bottom and Paradise Valley in Detroit.

Building freeways caused residents in African American neighborhoods to be displaced, resulting in the loss of homes and businesses. Nonetheless, many families demonstrated resilience by standing up for their rights and establishing new communities elsewhere in the city. Although expanding the freeway network promoted economic growth and improved connectivity, it also highlighted social justice concerns and displacement challenges. Enhanced transportation infrastructure facilitated increased social and cultural interactions, paving the way for a more connected future.

The rise in automobile ownership led to challenges, including an increase in drunk-driving incidents. Innovations such as the Drunkometer, developed by Robert F. Borkenstein in the 1930s, laid the foundation for detection devices. Borkenstein developed the Breathalyzer, a simple device that used a chemical reaction to measure a person's blood alcohol level from their breath. It helped law enforcement catch intoxicated drivers, improving road safety by raising awareness and enabling widespread testing locations.

The invention of the Breathalyzer created a new human-machine dynamic in law enforcement by offering an objective, machine-generated measurement of intoxication that largely replaced police officers' subjective judgments. Essentially, the machine became an essential, non-human partner in the law enforcement process, providing a scientific foundation for arrests and fundamentally changing the relationship between the officer, the suspect, and the legal system.

Transistors, Television, and the Rise of the Middle Class

In the past, human operators were crucial for operating machines, whether overseeing factory machinery or inputting punch cards into early computers. Despite their sophistication, these machines were just tools driven by human skill and imagination, with their abilities constrained by what their operators could achieve. Human intelligence was paramount, while machines served as the workhorses of history, dependent on human effort and guidance.

Emerging, the transistor revolutionized radios, hearing aids, and early computers, replacing bulky vacuum tubes with sleek, powerful, and portable electronics. This era created a new middle class that embraced technological progress, marking a key turning point in history. The television industry exploded in the 1950s, moving from experimental devices to stylish sets in middle-class homes. Color TV excited viewers and encouraged studios to produce new content and ideas. Sitcoms, anthologies, and Westerns marked a golden age as TV became a regular part of everyday life.

Transistors and phosphor technology enhanced picture quality and color accuracy. Media giants like CBS, NBC, and Time, Inc., revolutionized news and entertainment delivery, bridging social class gaps and shaping popular culture. Replacing vacuum tubes with transistors revolutionized computing and electronics by meeting the demands for reliability and smaller size.

Early interest from the Department of Defense and NASA also funded research into compact, dependable components, accelerating miniaturization and manufacturing advancements for commercial applications. Marketing shifted focus from electronic parts to device features such as portability, reliability, and innovation enabled by smaller technology. The pocket radio became a breakthrough marketing tool.

Credit in America: Its Rise and Risks

Credit cards, introduced in the 1950s, gave consumers more financial freedom and convenience. The "buy now, pay later" concept became popular, but also increased credit card fraud and identity theft, leading law enforcement to develop new countermeasures. Advancements such as the pocket recorder transformed how people captured and stored information, proving beneficial to journalists, students, and professionals alike. These devices made it easier to save and refer to meaningful discussions and data.

The 1950s were a period of major growth for the automotive, banking, and restaurant industries. General Motors and Ford led the car industry, while Chase National Bank and Bank of America expanded their influence. Quick-service restaurant pioneers like McDonald's, Burger King, and KFC introduced new ideas and kept prices affordable.

Retailers such as Sears, Roebuck & Co., and Woolworth's focused on convenience and accessibility, becoming staples for American shoppers. The rise of the automobile industry drove the expansion of car dealerships, repair shops, and gas stations, further shaping the economic landscape.

Masaru Ibuka and Akio Morita established Sony in 1946 as Tokyo Tsushin Kogyo. Their 1955 Sony TR-55 transistor radio transformed personal entertainment. Its compact size and affordable price made it popular worldwide, establishing Sony's reputation. Building on its success in radios, Sony applied transistor and phosphor technology to television sets, enhancing picture quality and color. The company's innovative spirit and branding, reflected in the name "Sony," demonstrate its commitment to technological progress and user-friendly design.

How Automation Redefined Employment

The mid-20th-century labor landscape was a blend of tradition and technological progress. Manufacturing, agriculture, and mining remained the main employment sectors, with manufacturing employing about 25-27% of the population in 1950. While agricultural work continued its decline due to mechanization, the service sector showed signs of future growth. Unemployment rates fluctuated but stayed manageable, supported by postwar prosperity.

During this period, the advent of early computers and automation created new career opportunities. Electronic devices replaced tasks previously performed by human "computers," increasing the need for technicians, engineers, and programmers to develop, construct, and sustain these systems. These roles demanded solid analytical and technical expertise, marking a shift where human-machine interaction evolved from purely mechanical tasks to innovative forms of intelligence.

Automation and robotics changed the job market in the 1950s. Robots handled repetitive tasks on assembly lines, increasing efficiency but removing specific jobs. However, new roles appeared, such as robot technicians and programmers, reflecting the evolving nature of industry work. Innovations such as the pocket recorder and the black box also influenced employment, boosting demand for transcriptionists and data analysts. Despite worries about job losses and ethical concerns, the public welcomed technological progress, paving the way for more rapid advances in the years ahead.

In the 1950s, labor trends showed an economy focused on manual and industrial jobs. Manufacturing was the primary employer, though agriculture remained important, particularly in rural regions. Early automation reduced the need for manual labor in factories and boosted demand for specialized skills, such as those of electromechanical technicians, machinery operators, and early programmers. The rise of AI also pointed to the growth of computational theorists and systems analysts.

Early attempts to replicate human problem-solving in the 1950s formed the basis for artificial intelligence. In 1956, the Logic Theorist showcased AI's capability to solve mathematical problems. Expert systems employed rule-based techniques to simulate human expertise in fields like medical diagnosis and chess. While primitive by today's standards, these developments sparked interest and set the stage for rapid advances in AI. Progress in electronics, transportation, and AI fueled optimistic views about technology's impact on society.

In the 1950s, thinkers had differing views on intelligence. Discussions and research on artificial intelligence examined whether machines could go beyond simple calculations and learn and reason. These underdeveloped ideas sparked a significant shift in human interaction with machines. This quiet revolution led to the creation of new job types.

In the 1950s, discussions about artificial intelligence forecasted major shifts in the future of work. While the majority still worked in conventional industries, ideas about AI pointed to roles centered on intelligence, innovation, and complex teamwork between humans and machines. Universities and research institutions of that era laid the groundwork for careers in AI research, data science, and advanced software engineering. Nonetheless, most tasks remained reliant on mechanical tools and human supervision.

In the late 1950s, the invention of the transistor sparked a wave of rapid technological progress. The first personal computers appeared, mainly used by governments and large companies, although they were large and bulky. These early machines had basic artificial intelligence and advanced telecommunications, setting the stage for future innovations. While digital marketplaces were still just ideas, most families focused on new color TVs and radios, unaware of the digital revolution to come.

The late 1950s laid the foundation for the digital revolution, although its effects were not yet visible. People focused on consumer electronics and transportation—interstate highways and transistor radios were changing daily life. Early data processing and networking tests showed signs of future e-commerce and online communication, but these innovations remained out of reach for most for years.

The 1950s marked a turning point in how people worked and interacted with machines. It was a time that combined the everyday realities of human labor and mechanical assistance with exciting ideas about intelligent technology. New technology jobs appeared alongside older ones, and traditional ideas about AI helped create future jobs that require creativity, broad thinking, and innovation. This decade started a shift that would reshape work and set the stage for future technological advances.

5

Workforce Changes in the 1960s

T he 1960s marked a pivotal period in the evolving relationship between humans and machines, characterized by both optimism and concern. In the 1960s, a typical family day reflected postwar suburban ideals, the emerging youth counterculture, and the rise of consumerism. Although family roles remained traditional primarily, technological advances made daily life easier and introduced new entertainment options. Visionaries like J.C.R. Licklider imagined a future where computers would collaborate with humans, aiding in thinking, decision-making, and communication.

Human-Machine Relationships

Attitudes during this time ranged from excitement about technological advances to fears that machines would surpass humans or cause disasters, especially with the rise of automation and the development of complex systems like nuclear weapons. This period also saw the emergence of the "cyborg" concept, which highlighted the balance between technological progress and the perceived risks posed by machines. While these ideas sparked hope, they also generated fears that automation and complex systems like nuclear weapons could fail or that machines might take over.

Labor statistics from the 1960s reflected these evolving trends. There was a significant decline in traditional manufacturing jobs, driven by the rapid adoption of automation. Mass production, once the backbone of industrial economies, depended on advanced control systems and automated machinery. This shift caused widespread concern about job losses but also opened the door to new forms of employment.

Emergence of a New Skilled Workforce

As automation and complex computational systems became more prevalent, a new skilled workforce arose, specializing in operating, maintaining, and developing these technologies. Over the decade, roles such as computer programmers, systems analysts, and data processing technicians gained prominence—positions that were rare earlier. These jobs required higher education and specialized training, representing a notable shift in the skills needed for economic participation.

The workforce adjusted to automation, with some jobs replaced and others collaborating with machines. In the early years, automation focused on basic manufacturing and mainframe processing, which was less advanced than current systems. While specialized machinery made notable progress, early computers faced technological limitations. In 1961, the debut of Unimate, the first industrial robot, on a General Motors assembly line marked a significant milestone in manufacturing efficiency. It handled repetitive tasks such as welding and spray painting, and factories used automated machines that, although controlled, still needed human oversight.

During this period, computers were large, expensive mainframes like the IBM System/360, used by large businesses and government agencies for data management and scientific research. The invention of the integrated circuit made electronic devices smaller and more accessible. Office environments also evolved with the adoption of electronic data processing, which transformed paper records into digital databases.

In homes, electric appliances like automatic washing machines became common, and microwave ovens helped automate basic household chores. However, automation mainly stayed in factories and blue-collar workplaces, focused on replacing simple, repetitive manual labor.

From Mechanization to Autonomous Systems

Transforming dedicated, hardware-based automation from the 1960s into today's interconnected, intelligent systems marks a significant evolution. Modern automation employs robotics, AI, machine learning, and IoT to handle complex tasks, in contrast to the limited mechanization of earlier decades.

Robert Noyce and Jack Kilby invented the microchip in 1959, igniting the development of integrated Circuits in the 1960s, which marked a breakthrough. This advancement transformed devices and systems, leading to innovations such as the first electronic desktop calculator in 1963 and the Apollo Guidance Computer used on Apollo missions. Microchips allowed computers to become smaller, faster, and more accessible, replacing large machines with compact models for homes and workplaces.

The integrated circuit (IC), or microchip, revolutionized the human-machine relationship not only by miniaturizing electronics but also by changing how we interact with technology through ubiquity, immediacy, and a shift from passive use to ongoing engagement. Before ICs, computers were large, expensive, and operated by trained personnel to handle complex batch tasks in isolation. The IC transformed this by enabling powerful, compact, affordable, and reliable computing that has become part of everyday life.

This shift affected the human-machine relationship in many ways, enabling devices such as personal computers and smartphones. Instead of interacting with machines at data centers as trained operators, these devices became accessible in homes, schools, and pockets worldwide, democratizing access to information and transforming users from specialists into everyday people.

Initially, computers processed data in batches, delivering results hours or even days later. The development of integrated circuit (IC) technology increased processing speeds, enabling real-time, interactive computing. Links now open instantly, and intelligent assistants respond right away. This speed has raised expectations for task completion and information access.

Before the advent of microchips, machines required manual operation of purpose-built devices, such as a washing machine with a timer. Currently, integrated circuits (ICs) enable machines to sense their environment, process intricate data, and function autonomously. Humans now rely on innovative, context-aware technologies—such as energy-saving thermostats and GPS rerouting—to perform tasks instead of doing them directly. The machine transformed into an all-encompassing assistant instead of merely a tool. During this time, simple graphics-based video games and the earliest types of interactive entertainment also emerged.

Technological Endeavors and Societal Impact

The 1960s experienced bold advances in technology, with the Space Race between the United States and the Soviet Union taking center stage. This rivalry propelled rapid progress in rocketry, materials science, and telecommunications, culminating in the 1969 moon landing—an impressive example of humans and machines working together.

Computers evolved from large mainframes that filled entire rooms to more advanced systems used in scientific and military fields. The invention of integrated circuits made them smaller and more powerful. Although most people still had limited direct access, technology's impact on society grew through improved infrastructure, faster communication, and advances in research. This period signaled both bold innovation and the ongoing integration of computing into essential daily activities.

According to the U.S. Bureau of Labor Statistics, U.S. manufacturing employment declined in the 1960s due to increased automation. As machines became more efficient and affordable, the demand for manual labor and repetitive tasks decreased, leading to significant changes in communities that relied on industrial jobs. Advances in computing introduced new job categories that needed skills that were scarce or nonexistent. The NSF emphasized the growing need for these skills and the importance of proper training. These technological advances changed human roles and economic outlooks, setting the stage for the digital age.

China's Control Over Rare Earth

Rare earth elements (REEs) are 17 metals vital to modern high-tech industries due to their fluorescent, conductive, and magnetic properties. Although not scarce, they are widely dispersed and challenging to refine. REEs are essential in small quantities for many common and specialized applications and technologies.

Extracting rare earths involves several steps and produces hazardous waste, including radioactive water, toxic acids, and heavy metals. Lanthanum is used in camera lenses, while yttrium and europium serve as phosphors for LED screens and lights.

In the 1960s, Chinese officials studied U.S. mining methods and created a cheaper way to process rare earths using plastic vats and hydrochloric acid. Along with plentiful resources, low labor costs, and few environmental regulations, this enabled China to lead the global rare-earth market at low prices.

The closure of Western rare-earth mines and processing plants in the late 1990s and early 2000s led to China's dominance of the market, causing price swings and heightened geopolitical risks. As Western companies pulled back, China solidified its control over the rare earth supply chain, now handling over 90% of global processing. As a result, the U.S. and Europe lost crucial expertise and infrastructure for advanced processing techniques such as solvent extraction.

Enterprises in sectors dependent on rare earth elements—such as magnet manufacturing for hard drives and electric vehicles—relocated their production facilities to China to secure access to affordable and reliable raw materials. This strategic decision has reinforced China's crucial role in the global manufacturing landscape, while the concentration of supply has introduced significant risks for countries that rely on its imports.

China gained significant geopolitical and economic influence by controlling vital minerals, which it can use in international negotiations or trade disputes. This shift turned the commercial market into a national security concern for Western countries. As a result, the competitive balance and resilience of the global market decreased, unintentionally ceding control over key high-tech resources to a single state actor.

A Decade of Transformation

The main story of the 1960s centers on inevitable changes. Research and industry reveal shared hopes for human-machine collaboration. Despite ongoing concerns about machine control, advancements in areas like rocketry and computing are evident. People have started integrating technology into their daily work, making the concept of a "cyborg" feel closer to reality. Reports from the US, including data from the Bureau of Labor Statistics and the National Science Foundation, show a society adapting to innovation and preparing for a digital era that will shape future decades.

6

Personal Computing in the 1970s

B etween 1960 and 1975, technology saw significant advancements: the space race reached its peak with the 1969 Apollo 11 moon landing, and inventions like the electronic wristwatch, pocket calculator, and early mobile phones emerged. CT scanning revolutionized medical diagnostics, while breakthroughs in fiber optics laid the foundation for future telecommunications. This era was marked by optimism and progress, as microchips became essential to many everyday items, such as cars and cameras, shaping modern technological life.

The main goal of the 1970s digital revolution was to democratize computing, moving technology from large, inaccessible institutions to individual users, encouraging creativity and connectivity. While engineers concentrated on miniaturizing computers, a counter-cultural movement recognized the potential for personal freedom. This inspired groups like the Homebrew Computer Club. Although the aim was to develop empowering personal devices, significant ethical questions arose about control and access to influence.

In the 1970s, a typical family day was heavily influenced by changing social norms, the expansion of suburbia, and the rise of consumer electronics. While traditional gender roles continued in many households, the decade also saw the rise of second cars, color televisions as the centerpiece of family entertainment, and the emergence of home computing and video games.

The 1970s also witnessed the emergence of video games, with the Magnavox Odyssey home console launching in 1972. Personal computers appeared with the Altair 8800 in 1975. These innovations showcased society's growing embrace of technology and marked the beginning of the digital age. The transition into the 1970s marked further evolution, with continued integration of automobiles, television culture, and advances in computing and networking. The foundation established during this time would lead to a different technological landscape, shaping the world for future generations.

In the 1970s, technological innovation grew rapidly worldwide, especially in entertainment. Automation now dominates manufacturing, with robots and software handling tasks like data entry and error detection. Modern automation includes AI for content creation, decision-making, and collaborative robots working alongside humans. Mattel kept Barbie popular with technology and accessories, Hasbro launched Transformers to increase interest in robots, and Lego inspired creativity. Meanwhile, automation mainly involves industrial machines and basic controls.

Work and Life in the 1970s

Automation is now everywhere—ubiquitous, intelligent, and connected. Since the 1970s, robotics like Unimate have enhanced efficiency, and PLCs and DCS systems have boosted reliability. Mainframes remained large and expensive, mainly used for data processing, while early home automation devices like X10 offered basic lighting, security, and thermostat control.

The 1970s introduced significant technological advances, especially in entertainment, merging creativity with technology to sustain Barbie's popularity and boost play with Transformers and Lego, inspiring future architects. Automation began with industrial machinery and has since become common, intelligent, and connected, embedded across many industries.

Gadgets such as electronic wristwatches, pocket calculators, and the first mobile phones debuted. CT scans revolutionized medical diagnostics, while breakthroughs in fiber optics paved the way for modern telecommunications. It was a period filled with optimism and rapid progress.

As the decade progressed, microchips became an essential part of daily items, from cars to cameras, influencing many areas of modern life. The 1970s also saw the rise of video games, with the Magnavox Odyssey home console debuting in 1972. Personal computers emerged with the Altair 8800 in 1975. These advances reflected society's increasing acceptance of technology and marked the start of the digital age.

New jobs required more intellectual involvement and closer teamwork with machines, indicating a significant shift in economic participation. Labor statistics from this period highlighted not only job losses but also innovations and the growth of a professional class linked to the digital age. Over the decade, labor data showed a notable decline in manufacturing sectors such as automotive, steel, and textiles due to advanced automation, leading to millions of job losses.

At the same time, new roles such as computer programmers, systems analysts, and data processing technicians emerged, requiring higher education and analytical skills. This shift changed the criteria for economic success, creating a gap between skilled workers and those without such skills and qualifications.

By 1975, a new era of technological advancement had started. The vehicles on the streets showcased futuristic designs with sharp angles and bright colors, while music shifted to include synthetic sounds and electronic beats. However, technology underwent the most remarkable revolution.

In 1975, the cultural landscape was lively. Gerald Ford was the U.S. President, focusing on economic recovery and political integrity. The entertainment industry prospered with blockbuster hits like "Jaws," ushering in a new era of summer films. Disco music's popularity soared, and rock bands like Led Zeppelin and the Rolling Stones reached their peak.

1975 marked a peak in culture and technology. Music blended electronic and natural sounds, exemplified by Captain & Tennille's hit "Love Will Keep Us Together," which topped charts. The automotive industry echoed the era's sleek style, with popular models like the Chevrolet Caprice and Ford LTD combining fashion with practicality.

By 1978, imagination and technology merged in the toy industry. Mattel's

Barbie grew with new accessories, while Hasbro's Transformers engaged children with intricate storylines. Lego continued to inspire creativity, and Kenner Products launched Star Wars action figures, linking toys to Hollywood blockbusters.

The entertainment industry thrived with iconic films like "Grease" and "Superman." Disco music soared to new heights, while punk and new wave genres challenged mainstream sounds. Technology, media, and creativity shaped the generation's trends and tastes. Films influenced how people viewed technology by vividly depicting possible computer worlds, even though few had real-life experience with computers.

A New Class of Wealth

During the late 1970s, technology advanced significantly. In 1979, Sony launched the Walkman, changing how people listened to music by letting them carry their favorite songs anywhere. Powerful microprocessors such as the Intel 8086 and Motorola 68000 emerged, driving the computing revolution and enabling personal computers. The Apple II, released in 1977, and the IBM PC, introduced in 1981, became iconic and brought computing into homes.

In the late 1970s, electronics giants like Sony and JVC gained fame, transforming the industry for years to come. Sony's Walkman became a cultural icon, blending technology with entertainment, while JVC's VCR revolutionized media consumption. The Walkman's sleek design and features made it a cultural icon. The VCR transformed home entertainment, allowing viewers to record and replay TV shows, with brands like JVC and Philips giving them unprecedented control over their viewing experience.

The wealthiest people in the United States reflected the changing industrial landscape. Tech entrepreneurs like Bill Gates emerged among the country's most prosperous, signaling the rise of technology-driven fortunes. Established families, such as the Waltons of Walmart and the Mars family of Mars candy, continued to dominate the retail and candy industries.

Late 1970s housing reflected both aesthetic and technological advances.

Split-level homes, featuring multiple floors and partial staircases, became popular, moving away from the ranch-style homes of earlier decades. Exteriors often used wood and brick for warmth and visual appeal, with large windows that increased natural light and merged indoor and outdoor spaces.

New technologies in home building included energy-efficient features and the early adoption of "smart" home systems. Solar panels, though still new, appeared on roofs to harness solar energy. Early smart thermostats and security systems gave homeowners better control and convenience, reflecting a growing focus on energy conservation and technological integration.

During this period, home prices ranged from $50,000 to $70,000, with larger or luxury properties surpassing this range. Education underwent notable changes, emphasizing vocational and technical training to adapt to a changing job market and new industries. Community colleges and vocational schools gained popularity by offering programs in electronics, computer science, and business.

As the technology and business sectors expanded, computer programmers, electronics engineers, and marketing professionals occupied the most in-demand positions. Traditional industries like manufacturing and heavy industry declined due to automation and outsourcing.

Machines, Movies, and Meals

The technology sector, including electronics, computers, and software, led by companies like Microsoft and Apple, was at the forefront of industry growth. The entertainment industry, driven by Hollywood and the music business, thrived, while fast food expanded, with McDonald's and Burger King as major players. Declining industries included agriculture, textiles, and steel, which faced challenges from automation, outsourcing, and foreign competition.

McDonald's has positioned itself as a leader in the fast-food industry, with the Golden Arches becoming a widely recognized symbol. The Big Mac has grown into a cultural icon, just as Levi Strauss & Co.'s denim jeans and jackets have become staple wardrobe pieces for many generations, representing both durability and timeless fashion.

Cultural trends—blending synthetic and organic music, hit movies, and evolving fashion—laid the foundation for the technological breakthroughs of the next decade. The economy, fueled by new tech innovators and established retail giants, pointed toward a future focused on digital advancement.

In 1970, automation was mainly a niche tool for heavy industries. Now, it has evolved into an interconnected, intelligent system transforming sectors and lifestyles, ultimately shaping the world. The emergence of personal computers in the 1970s signaled a significant change in the relationship between humans and technology. For the first time, designers prioritized individual users when creating advanced computing devices.

Hobbyist kits and early commercial machines, such as the Apple II and Commodore PET, emerged, though they still required some technical skills. During this decade, computing began to move out of specialized labs and into homes and small businesses.

Telecommunications technology advanced, with improvements in telephone networks and the early development of packet switching—a precursor to the internet. The way humans interacted with technology shifted from passive consumption of mass media to more active engagement with computational tools, though only among a niche audience.

The idea of a "computer on every desk" saw technology as both a personal assistant and a creative tool, not just an industrial device or a broadcast medium. It represented a move towards personal empowerment through technology.

The Algorithm of Employment

While the rise of personal computers sparked excitement and the hope of individual empowerment, it also cast a shadow over established labor structures. Moving computing power from labs to homes and small businesses highlighted automation's impact on employment.

For some, the personal computer was a creative tool or personal assistant; for others, it indicated the potential for job displacement. Although it is difficult to pinpoint precise labor statistics tracking the impact of personal computers and automation on job creation and loss in the early 1970s, broader trends provide insight.

The demand for computer programmers, systems analysts, and data entry personnel, though limited in the early 1970s, grew as businesses of all sizes adopted these new machines. Manufacturing personal computers also created assembly line jobs, adding a technological element to familiar industrial models. According to the Bureau of Labor Statistics, the U.S. civilian labor force grew from 87 million in 1970 to over 100 million by 1979. This increase reflects economic growth, but it also masks underlying shifts driven by the introduction of computing tools that have created new job roles.

Job displacement originated in industries that depended on manual calculations and repetitive administrative work. Positions like bookkeepers, typists, and filing clerks, once widespread, became outdated as personal computers offered faster digital alternatives. Early word-processing software reduced the need for typists and shorthand secretaries. Simultaneously, early databases and accounting programs handled information more quickly than manual approaches, rendering traditional data clerks unnecessary.

Moving from passive use to active engagement with computing tools enabled individuals and revolutionized industries reliant on traditional methods, such as print media and advertising. While detailed data on job losses caused by personal computer automation in the 1970s is limited, that era laid the foundation for later advances in workplace efficiency. The transition happened gradually, as experienced hobbyists mainly used early machines and kits.

While employment levels remained steady, advances in technology increased individual autonomy, thereby reducing the need for specific skills and roles. Improvements in telecommunications, such as enhanced telephone networks and early packet switching, heightened the potential for change, suggesting a future where communication and information processing would transform industries beyond personal computing. During that decade, computing's power influenced work and livelihoods.

Introducing the New Desk Job

Integrating personal computers into daily life beyond laboratories transformed employment, leading to increased women's participation in the labor force over the decade. Simultaneously, new job roles emerged to meet technical demands, such as computer repair technicians, early software developers, and data entry specialists. These positions supported the growing need to build, maintain, and operate accessible computing devices. Meanwhile, automation challenged traditional roles, especially those involving repetitive data processing and record-keeping.

The idea of "a computer on every desk" envisioned a future where machines could perform tasks faster, reducing the need for human labor in specific roles and shifting reliance to adaptable individuals. Job creation and the potential for job elimination interacted during this period, a trend that would grow as technological advancements advanced. Although early labor statistics did not reflect the digital revolution's impact, they did show signs of transformation.

Advances in telecommunications and personal computing weren't just technological breakthroughs — they changed the way people work. Those who adapted found new opportunities and felt more empowered by technology, while others faced uncertainty as automation spread. Digital tools, which simplified workflows and increased efficiency, gradually replaced manual clerical and administrative roles.

Demand for technical professionals—such as electronics technicians, computer programmers, and systems analysts—increased as their skills became essential. Turning passive consumption into active engagement was not only a philosophical shift but also an economic one, making technological literacy a crucial factor for employment.

As automation transformed industries reliant on large-scale computing and mechanical systems, personal computers introduced new jobs—such as device assembly, repair, software development, and tech support. This crucial shift led technology to replace some roles while also creating new ones, fueled by rapid innovation and greater personal access.

The shift toward personal empowerment through technology changed job-market demands. The concept of having a "computer on every desk" meant workers needed to become more proficient with digital tools. Schools and training programs began adjusting, mainly to help people develop these skills.

Early machines required advanced technical skills, highlighting the growing need for digital expertise. Although the exact job losses caused by personal computers in the 1970s are unclear, increased automation and the rise of computer-focused roles marked significant workforce changes.

Building the Digital Workforce

In the 1970s, artificial intelligence had little measured effect on employment; job reductions were mainly due to early automation and computing. AI job displacement was mostly theoretical, as technological efficiencies—not advanced algorithms—drove change. Automation, especially with computers in industry, reduced the need for humans in repetitive tasks.

In administration, early word processing and database programs made tasks more manageable, changing roles in data entry and secretarial work. New opportunities in the personal computer industry, from repair technicians to early software developers and electronics assemblers, indicate a shift in valued skills.

A critical turning point occurred in the 1970s as computing's potential began to affect work. Additionally, technology challenged employment by enabling individuals. The pace of change accelerated. As it developed, some people adjusted quickly. The main idea was straightforward: moving toward personal empowerment meant that specific skills and roles would become less critical. Thanks to advances in telecommunications and personal computers, this shift accelerated, transforming how we communicate, process information, and perceive work.

The 1970s marked a turning point in human-technology relations, driven by increased access to computing and early automation in the workforce. The shift from passive consumption to active participation empowered some but also prompted a reassessment of skills and careers.

Although early labor data didn't capture the impact of personal computers, the shift to tech-driven efficiency began reshaping employment, creating new technical jobs and displacing manual process sectors. Establishing a new paradigm is where the legacy of the 1970s lies. Seeing a "computer on every desk," though not yet realized, signaled a future in which technology would be central to productivity and creativity, with dependency shifting toward personal empowerment.

The era emphasized digital literacy and adaptability as essential skills for a workforce in a changing world, driven by computing technology. As the 1970s concluded, society was entering a new decade marked by technological and cultural shifts. The electronics industry paved the way for the digital age, and the wealthiest Americans embodied the spirit of innovation and entrepreneurship.

III

Digital Revolution Unfolds (1980s-2020s)

Part 3 summarizes the key technological advances from the 1980s to the early 2020s and their societal impact, supported by historical examples and economic data, including references from the U.S. Bureau of Labor Statistics. Using a chronological approach, it examines technology's influence on society, the economy, the labor market, and public health, highlighting examples such as Apollo 11, Altair 8800, Sony Walkman, and IBM PC.

7

The Digital Revolution of the 1980s

I n the 1980s, families saw rising dual incomes and expanded use of consumer electronics, which fostered digital habits. Automation began with costly factory systems and early computers, evolving into today's widespread AI and IoT solutions. Early innovations like Unimate, though reliant on skilled operators and prone to reliability issues, significantly impacted manufacturing in the automotive industry.

Over the decade, offices moved from paper files to digital databases. Fax machines and answering machines became common, while affordable personal computers allowed more people to use word processing and basic data management. These early computers had limited hardware, no networking, and were starting to adopt graphical user interfaces. Home automation was uncommon, with wired systems like X10 being rugged to install.

From Assembly Line to Smart Home

By 1980, the U.S. housing market had changed significantly. With mortgage rates around 12%, many buyers moved to the suburbs, creating new opportunities for families. During the boom, low interest rates made buying homes affordable, leading families to seek larger houses with yards, which shifted the meaning of "home" and expanded family dreams. The real estate market in the 1980s faced both opportunities and challenges due to economic shifts and fluctuating interest rates, which affected mortgage costs.

Single-family homes were the most common, but apartments and condos grew in popularity, especially in cities. Ranch-style houses, with their single-story layouts and open floor plans, were favorites. Split-level and multi-story homes appealed to those seeking more space. As technology advanced, some houses featured early automation systems for lighting, security, and climate control.

The new decade ushered in significant changes to the automotive industry. Vehicles symbolised status and innovation. Electronic fuel injection boosted engine performance and efficiency. Cassette decks developed into complete entertainment systems for on-the-go music.

The 1980s saw significant advances in car safety, with features like anti-lock brakes, seat belts promoted through public campaigns, and airbags demonstrating the industry's commitment to protecting drivers. Car designs also changed, adopting sleek, aerodynamic styles that replaced the boxy shapes of the 70s. Streamlined appearances and stylish touches, such as pop-up headlights, reflected the decade's forward-looking spirit, making it a golden era when style, performance, and technology came together.

Fashion and Entertainment, Travel and Tourism

The 1980s marked a shift away from the disco era, emphasizing innovation and technological advances. Fashion became bold, featuring bright colors and unique shapes, such as shoulder pads and oversized sleeves. Social interactions evolved as personal computers became common at home, transforming work, leisure, and connectivity.

Fast-food giants like McDonald's, Burger King, and Wendy's dominated the mid-80s scene, with Happy Meals costing about $1.50 to $2.00 and including toys—something new. Iconic bands and artists such as Duran Duran, A-ha, Wham!, Madonna, and Prince shaped the decade's musical and cultural identity.

Travel and tourism expanded during the 1980s. Domestic travel within the United States became popular, with families visiting national parks such as the Grand Canyon and Yellowstone. Camping and road trips became affordable ways to explore the country's diverse landscapes.

For tropical escapes, the Caribbean islands feature all-inclusive resorts in Jamaica, the Bahamas, and the Dominican Republic, with prices beginning at approximately $50 per person per night. Urban exploration in New York City is equally budget-friendly, with round-trip flights starting at $150 and affordable lodging ranging from $40 to $50 per night.

The Revolution in Personal Computing

The 1980s marked a turning point with the rise of personal computers, changing both work and home life. Iconic devices like IBM's PC and Apple's Macintosh introduced graphical interfaces into everyday life, making computers more user-friendly. As tools like word processors, spreadsheets, and databases became standard, productivity improved.

The debut of the first Apple Macintosh further expanded computer accessibility by providing user-friendly interfaces and graphical features to a broader audience. These computers fostered creativity and productivity through functions like word processing, gaming, and early online communication. Although concerns about privacy and misuse emerged, personal computers quickly became vital in homes and workplaces. A combination of public investment, private-sector competition, and evolving user needs shaped the path of the digital revolution.

Video games grew into a booming industry, with titles like "Pac-Man," "Space Invaders," and "Super Mario Bros." becoming household names. Early computer graphics brought movies like "Tron" to life, blending technology and pop culture. Innovations in films like Tron shaped how the public viewed technology by providing a visually striking, imaginative look at a potential "computer world" at a time when most people had limited exposure to computers. The film helped turn an abstract idea into a vivid, accessible, and exciting visual experience.

The concept of networking grew as LANs developed in businesses, enabling resource sharing. While the internet was still in its early stages, online services and BBSs pointed to a connected future. A shift in the relationship between humans and technology—where computers evolved from simple calculators to creative tools, communication devices, and gateways to vast information—defined this period. People and organizations began relying more on these digital tools for everyday tasks and personal use activities.

During this period, popular electronics included personal computers, videocassette recorders (VCRs), and boom boxes. The personal computer became a household staple, providing word processing, gaming, and early online communication. The VCR transformed home entertainment, while the boombox became a symbol of youth culture.

Home appliances emphasized convenience, introducing feature-rich microwave ovens, dishwashers, and refrigerators, while energy-efficient washing machines and dryers became widespread. In the 1980s, telecommunications underwent significant changes: landline phones became common in homes and businesses, enabling instant long-distance calls. The first cellular network call in 1983 signaled the start of wireless communication. Also, fax machines and car phones emerged, revolutionizing document sharing and mobile communication.

Charting Careers in a Computerized World

The 1980s personal computing revolution changed the way we work and the job market. Despite complex labor statistics, there's a notable rise in digital-related jobs. Roles like programmers, analysts, and data clerks became highly sought, forming new career paths requiring tech knowledge that didn't exist a decade earlier, shaping the technological backbone revolution.

The rise of user-friendly computers increased demand for technical support and trainers, diversifying the job market. Networking created roles for network administrators and technicians to meet organizational needs. While productivity increased, traditional clerical roles such as typists and clerks declined as software and digital databases automated many obsolete manual tasks.

Those involved in the production and distribution of documents, such as typesetters, and the rise of digital publishing, affected some printing press operators. The labor market underwent a steady recalibration, with once-essential manual or paper-based skills losing value amid automation and advanced software. The growing dependency on digital tools required a workforce capable of managing and interacting with them, leaving behind those whose skill sets did not adapt.

This decade saw the rise of new vocational fields, often requiring specialized knowledge of software and hardware. Computer programmers, systems analysts, and data entry clerks became essential for digital infrastructure. User-friendly graphical interfaces increased demand for support and training, bridging knowledge gaps and boosting adoption—networking technologies such as LANs created roles for network administrators and technicians.

Early analyses, including those by the Bureau of Labor Statistics, began tracking the rise of computer-related jobs and the decline of specific administrative support roles. However, detailed data on job losses caused by automation only emerged in later decades as these trends became clearer. Automation, driven by advanced software, has replaced workers in repetitive and predictable roles, especially in clerical work.

Word processors replaced manual typing and editing, and database management simplified administrative tasks. While job loss data from automation reflects broader employment trends, the cause was clear: skills linked to manual or paper-based work lost value, prompting workers to reskill and adapt. This period sparked a careful balance between human labor and technology, leading to a new outlook on workforce capabilities.

As digital tools became widespread, the meaning of "work" expanded beyond performing tasks to include managing and utilizing information. Although these tools empower users, they also generate concerns about job security and the changing nature of employment. Early online platforms and BBSs offered glimpses of a future with increased access to information, indicating shifts in knowledge work and fields such as librarianship as they began to adapt to digital archives and information retrieval.

Artificial intelligence became a practical reality in the 1980s. During that time, older AI technologies, such as expert systems and methods for human language understanding, were innovative, even though they now seem pretty basic. Expert systems aim to replicate human decision-making, and people use them in medical diagnosis, language interpretation, and gaming.

These innovations laid the groundwork for future intelligent technologies. Personal computers kept improving, and the concept of the Internet started to take shape. The 1980s marked the end of the first phase of the information age, leading to a period characterized by increased connectivity and digital transformation.

Expert systems mimicked human decision-making, used in medical diagnosis, translation, and gaming. These advancements led to more sophisticated intelligent systems. Personal computers evolved alongside the Internet. By the 1980s, these advances laid the foundation for the information age, boosting connectivity and digital transformation. Automation-enhanced dialers and 911 dispatch centers, while early AI in manufacturing, military, healthcare, and finance paved the way for greater human integration with machines.

Navigating the New Economy

The personal computer revolution changed the job market in the 1980s. There was a rising demand for programmers, software developers, and computer engineers, leading many to improve and develop their skills. However, the tech industry mainly favored White professionals, who had better access to education and training, thus maintaining existing inequalities.

Traditional blue-collar jobs persisted, but the growing service sector—including finance, consulting, and sales—became more appealing. Prestigious universities like Harvard, Yale, and MIT continued to develop leaders, while specialized science and engineering schools such as MIT, Caltech, and Carnegie Mellon gained prominence, influencing the tech industry.

Due to high costs, many low-income families could not afford computers, widening the digital divide. As personal computers became more widespread, new health concerns emerged, including musculoskeletal problems such as carpal tunnel syndrome, as ergonomic solutions were still developing. The shift away from physically demanding jobs also brought new workplace health issues.

Mentally, the constant flow of information and multitasking enabled by computers can break attention spans and hinder deep focus. Physically, problems like carpal tunnel syndrome were common before ergonomic solutions became widespread. As computers became essential for accessing information and solving problems, concerns grew about over-reliance on machines, which could diminish critical thinking and memory.

The comfort with digital environments also influenced social interactions, as early online platforms provided alternatives to face-to-face communication. While personal empowerment and efficiency increased, dependence on technology subtly led to physical and cognitive health issues that require ongoing attention as technology becomes more embedded in daily life.

From Disco to Digital

By the late 1980s, emerging technologies were beginning to shape the future. In 1989, Tim Berners-Lee invented the World Wide Web, igniting a revolution in information sharing. That same year, Casio introduced its first handheld personal organizer, the DA-2. The NES, which boosted the home video game industry in 1985, featured iconic characters that became cultural symbols. Meanwhile, personal computers and networking technology started transforming homes and businesses, laying the groundwork for online commerce and global connectivity.

1980 marked a shift from 70s disco. As the decade began, American families faced rising grocery bills and had to adapt to economic changes. Early online services and bulletin boards started connecting users and building communities, hinting at an interconnected future. Software evolved, with more user-friendly operating systems and expanding applications, laying the groundwork for the digital revolution of the 1990s.

In the 1980s, basic services such as banking and shopping evolved with the rise of automated systems and early online transactions. This decade laid the foundation for a future where technology became an essential part of daily life, sparking a new era of connectivity and innovation. Healthcare and basic services also benefited from technological progress. Medical professionals adopted new procedures and equipment, improving diagnosis and treatment options. Computers became common in healthcare settings, supporting record-keeping, data management, and analysis.

Automation today is widespread, intelligent, and connected, shaping both industry and daily life. It now includes thermostats and security systems. Modern systems can process large datasets, recognize patterns, learn from experience, and make complex decisions that usually require human expertise. Devices and systems connect via the internet and wireless protocols, enabling seamless integration and centralized management.

With on-demand computing making automation more scalable, organizations of all sizes can now handle complex tasks like GPS navigation, legal document processing, and supply chain optimization. Automation has evolved from basic functions to intelligent, interconnected systems that learn and improve, leading to unprecedented efficiency and capability since 1980.

The 1980s laid the groundwork for a society that became increasingly dependent on technology. By the end of the decade, personal computers had become integral to daily life, driving ongoing change and raising important questions about the long-term impact of technology on work and health. Although these innovations boosted productivity and empowerment, they also created new job opportunities while making others obsolete, posing new challenges to well-being. The warning lights indicating the pot was overheating were now flashing orange rapidly.

8

The Digital Influence of the 1990s

The 1990s saw explosive growth in the Internet, transforming it from an academic and military tool into a global phenomenon. Tim Berners-Lee's HTML, URLs, and HTTP enabled navigable websites, while browsers like Netscape made the Internet accessible to all. Family activities changed as technology allowed more personalized access to entertainment and information. Early shared experiences shifted as the Internet and personal devices increasingly created digital divisions in households.

This decade saw a surge of online users and content, fueling the dot-com boom. E-commerce expanded, email became essential, personal computers became household staples, and the Internet was known as the "information superhighway." Humans increasingly relied on technology for information, communication, and daily needs. Optimism about rapid integration marked this era, as technology transformed social life and the global economy.

From Analog to Automated

In 1990, automation depended on specialized industrial machines and basic computerized office systems. In manufacturing, industrial robots handled tasks like welding and painting, increasing productivity, but still needing manual setup and supervision. Offices began digitizing records and using personal computers with simple software, while early business process management (BPM) systems appeared.

Home automation was rare, expensive, and complicated at that time, making it out of reach for most households. With the Internet just starting to develop, real-time communication between devices was limited and still experimental. By the 1990s, food prices had become a significant concern for families. A dozen eggs, which cost less than $1 in the 1980s, now exceeded $1.50, and ground beef averaged about $2.50 per pound. Families adjusted their budgets to make sure they could afford their basic needs.

American life during this period reflected a growing fascination with digital innovation. For example, a Happy Meal costs $2.99 and remains a favorite treat for kids because of its toy surprise. The Dallas Cowboys won the Super Bowl in 1994, capturing national attention and showcasing the era's enthusiasm for sports and entertainment. These details demonstrate how technological progress and economic realities influenced everyday life in the United States.

The 1990s saw a mix of analog and digital technologies, with rapid innovations that impacted all aspects of society. The growth of the Internet and early AI projects shifted daily routines, bringing AI from concepts to real-world applications in manufacturing and basic smart home technology. In 1992, expanding Internet infrastructure and easier access to personal computers heightened excitement about the potential to transform communication and information access.

As mobile phones became sleeker and more integrated, machines helped analyze and predict user needs, laying the groundwork for a hyper-connected, AI-driven future. By 1992, the expanding Internet generated vast amounts of data, leading to early AI systems, such as data-mining algorithms, that identified trends, influenced marketing and research, and paved the way for personalized digital experiences. Although analog traditions persisted, digital innovation accelerated, transforming American life. Everyday concerns like grocery prices and family plans remained important even as technology promised to improve daily life routines.

The Digital Divide

The 1990s Internet boom significantly impacted society, making the Web a household and business staple. Communication changed with the rise of faster email and messaging. Economic growth, with mortgage rates falling from 8% to 6.5%, eased homeownership and boosted real estate. An improved economy also fueled tech adoption, as Americans had more disposable income to buy computers and use online services.

In real estate, the idea of the "smart home" has become popular, with new houses featuring open layouts, high ceilings, large windows, and versatile living spaces that adapt to changing household needs. The growth of technology and automation has changed domestic living. The expansion of the Internet led to a surge in gadgets and electronics. Portable CD players allowed music lovers to enjoy their favorite tunes anywhere. At the same time, video game consoles such as the Super Nintendo and Sega Genesis introduced players to interactive experiences and storytelling.

Today's home appliances include refrigerators with recipe and grocery screens, voice-activated ovens and microwaves, and AI-powered cleaning robots that handle both vacuuming and mopping. These innovations demonstrate how AI has become a natural part of everyday technology, evolving from fixing errors in CD players to managing game logic in consoles. Now, appliances are learning user preferences, signaling the early stages of AI transforming household products and making home life more convenient.

Technology has transformed welfare systems through AI, streamlining assessments, reducing paperwork, and speeding access. However, bias and errors in automation raise ethical concerns. As the Internet grew, universities such as Stanford, MIT, and Carnegie Mellon focused on computer science and engineering, becoming hubs of innovation and preparing students for the digital age. Yet the skills gap widened as curricula lagged behind rapid technological advances.

Recognizing the societal impact of technology, universities began offering courses on ethics and the broader influence of innovation. Nonetheless, the digital divide persisted in education, with wealthy, predominantly white schools having better access to computers and the Internet, whereas under-resourced and minority-serving institutions fell behind. This ongoing disparity deepened existing inequalities. The release of Apple's iMac in 1998 helped close some of these gaps by making technology more accessible to a broader audience.

As technology advanced, disparities in access grew, with White Americans benefiting more from the digital revolution. Long-standing inequalities and systemic racism limited educational and resource opportunities for people of color, widening the 'digital divide.' Coined in the mid-1990s, the term refers to disparities by race and socioeconomic status. White Americans had better access to and job opportunities, while minorities often lacked digital skills. Incorporating technology into welfare could increase efficiency but might worsen inequalities if not carefully managed, as affordability and underfunded minority communities remain significant issues.

The digital divide goes beyond just access to technology and stems from deep-rooted inequalities such as housing discrimination, unequal education funding, and cultural biases in technology and internet development. Redlining, initiated by the HOLC in the 1930s, denied loans and insurance to Black and minority neighborhoods, causing long-term economic decline. Today, maps showing limited high-speed internet often mirror these old redlining boundaries, as service providers tend to avoid investing in less profitable areas—a trend called "digital" redlining.

Because public school funding depends on local property taxes, historically redlined neighborhoods have faced underfunded schools. As a result, there are fewer opportunities to access advanced courses and essential resources, such as modern technology and digital skills, which creates ongoing gaps in education and skills. Wealthy academics and researchers helped shape the early internet, developing tools and designs aligned with their norms, often excluding some groups and making adoption more difficult for less-educated individuals.

In the 1990s, as the internet became a commercial platform, its marketing and content reflected social inequalities. Early access needed costly computers and dial-up, so wealthier households were the primary users and targets.

Content focused on academic, technical, and e-commerce topics for wealthy Western audiences, making it less relevant to minorities and low-income groups. Beginning with the first banner ad in 1994, online advertising shifted to targeting affluent users. Consequently, content and services mainly suited those with disposable income, deepening disparities and the digital divide.

The Era of the Internet and AI

By 1992, the Internet was transitioning from being mainly used by academics and government agencies to becoming part of mainstream America. Dial-up modems allowed more households to connect to this expanding network, even though the technology remained basic. AI research in neural networks and machine learning has shown significant potential, with applications in data management and the development of future intelligent systems assistants.

Mobile phones became gateways to the Internet, marking the rise of an interconnected digital world. The passive information era ended, replaced by interactive, AI-driven engagement. Optimism in the 1990s, fueled by the internet's expansion, also affected the labor market. The "information superhighway" opened new avenues for commerce and communication, weakening traditional industries and changing work patterns. Employment data showed a sharp rise in technical roles such as web developers, network admins, and IT support staff, as companies rushed to build online presences.

This period saw a notable increase in overall employment, indicating a thriving economy adjusting to technological advancements. For instance, the U.S. Bureau of Labor Statistics (BLS) documented steady job growth during the 1990s, with the technology sector at the forefront. (U.S. Bureau of Labor Statistics, Employment and Earnings, Reports, 1990-1999).

The rising demand for new technical roles reflected a fundamental shift in the job market. While overall job growth was steady, much of it occurred in the digital sector, driven by the Web's commercialization. This fueled ongoing demand for professionals to build, maintain, and improve online infrastructure. Web developers, who create user-friendly and functional websites, have experienced an increase in demand.

Network administrators are vital to digital infrastructure, ensuring smooth data flow. IT support specialists, once niche, now act as frontline defenders against tech issues. The demand for these skills surpasses supply, driving fierce competition and higher salaries for specialists. This growth in tech has displaced traditional jobs; as e-commerce has grown, roles in retail sales, cash handling, and inventory have faced unprecedented declines.

Automation's Toll on Body and Soul

Automation has enhanced process efficiency, decreasing the need for large call centers, typesetters, and proofreaders. Digital publishing influences traditional media roles, showing how technology can be both helpful and problematic. Despite optimism about the "information superhighway," job changers faced underlying concerns.

Growth from 1990 to 1999, as shown by BLS and 'Employment and Earnings' data, reflected a workforce influenced by technology and outdated skills. The decade both created jobs and caused disruption, sparking debates about retraining and the future of digital employment. However, this rapid period of integration also had its costs. Automation fueling e-commerce and online services has displaced workers from traditional roles. As companies adopted more efficient, technology-driven methods, jobs involving manual labor or repetitive tasks in manufacturing, clerical work, and retail declined.

Although it is difficult to determine the exact number of jobs lost to automation this decade, the trend was evident. The increasing use of the Internet for tasks such as order-taking and customer service indicates that human labor will shift more toward oversight, design, and specialized problem-solving rather than direct task execution.

This shift represented a significant change in reliance, moving from traditional jobs to roles that demand adaptability and continuous learning. (Autor, D. H. (2015). The widespread adoption of the Internet into daily life, known as the "information superhighway," altered human behavior and created a new dependence that led to unexpected physical effects. As the digital world provided ever-increasing convenience and instant gratification, physical activity declined.

The appeal of online shopping has led to fewer trips to crowded markets, reducing the incidental exercise of walking through aisles and carrying purchases. The rise of streaming services and online gaming has caused a decline in outdoor activities and physical hobbies. This shift toward a sedentary lifestyle, driven by the constant appeal of screens, has contributed to a nationwide increase in obesity and related health issues.

The Internet's increased accessibility revolutionized it but also resulted in higher inactivity levels compared to earlier generations (Kohl, H. W., & Potts, J. A., 1990; Hu, F.B., 1990). This reliance on technology has extended beyond convenience, becoming an integral part of daily routines and affecting physical health. By the late 1990s, PCs were widespread, encouraging more use and changing how people spent their time.

People's entertainment, socializing, and food ordering habits influence their dietary choices and exercise routines. Fast-food delivery, supported by new e-commerce platforms, offers an attractive alternative to traditional homemade meals that require physical preparation. Nutritional intake is often skewed toward processed, high-calorie options, which worsens the impact of reduced physical activity. This shift from active participation to passive digital consumption has created a public health crisis where technological advancements harm human health even as they offer benefits. (Hu, F. B. (2008). Diet, Lifestyle, and the Risk of Obesity. BMJ, 337 (aug14_1a1743.)

The strong bond between humans and technology in the 1990s, though celebrated for its benefits in information sharing and communication, subtly but significantly impacted metabolic health. Constant access to digital entertainment and the seamless integration of e-commerce into daily routines promoted a lifestyle marked by extended periods of sitting and inactivity.

Reduced physical activity and easier access to high-calorie foods online have led to weight gain and health problems like heart disease and diabetes. The "information superhighway" improved connectivity but also increased physical inactivity, prompting a reevaluation of its true impact. As reliance on the Internet increased, so did the use of physical tools, indicating early health challenges in the twenty-first century. (Sallis, J. F., Stark, B. L., & Kerr, J 2004)

Internet Use and the Public Health Crisis

Internet use is linked to more sedentary lifestyles, which increase obesity and metabolic disease rates. Numerous studies have shown a connection between internet use and adverse health outcomes, although this public health crisis is complex and multi-layered. Factors such as behavioral choices, environmental influences, and physiological responses all contribute to the problem, underscoring that technology use is not the only factor.

The widespread use of internet-connected devices, including computers, smartphones, and tablets, increases many people's daily screen time. Studies show that more screen time is associated with higher BMI and increased risk of overweight or obesity. Specifically, a systematic review and meta-analysis found a dose-response relationship: each additional hour of internet use per day was associated with an 8% increase in the odds of being overweight or obese.

Longitudinal studies have also shown strong links between extended screen time and changes in BMI, especially among teenagers. Those who spend four or more hours on screens each day are more likely to face weight issues and disrupted sleep patterns. High screen time often replaces essential health habits, such as physical activity and sufficient sleep, leading to an overall energy imbalance.

Extended internet use is associated with unhealthy eating habits, such as late-night meals and increased snacking on junk food. Exposure to targeted food advertising online can influence dietary preferences and choices. Research shows that adults who spend a lot of leisure time online are more likely to be obese, even if they stay physically active during their free time.

Prolonged sedentary behavior is an independent risk factor for obesity. While technology, including internet use, plays a role, it is only one factor in the rising obesity rates. Obesity results from both personal choices and environments that promote unhealthy habits. Effective solutions require comprehensive public health strategies and approaches.

The Workforce Shift of the 90s

Two major changes define the story of the 1990s. While personal computers and the Internet provided unprecedented access to information and fostered new connections, they also transformed the workforce. The optimism of the dot-com boom masked a deeper tension: the promise of new opportunities alongside the quiet decline of older ones. This period laid the groundwork for ongoing labor shifts, pushing society to confront the profound effects of technology on work and the global economy. This theme will remain significant in the coming decades.

The optimistic view from official labor statistics in the 1990s, which indicated strong economic growth, warrants a closer look to understand how the workforce truly evolved. The U.S. Bureau of Labor Statistics (BLS) consistently reported positive net job gains throughout the decade, often exceeding two million jobs annually. For instance, the BLS's "Employment and Earnings" reports showed growth in the service sector, primarily driven by expansion in information technology. Notably, certain occupations, such as computer and mathematical roles—like software developers and systems analysts—experienced substantial growth, with increases well above the national average.

Management, business, and financial occupations also experienced significant growth, driven by the need for strategic planning and implementation in this evolving economic environment. This period marked the emergence of professions that were either nonexistent or just beginning at the start of the decade. Web developers — the creators of the digital world — saw an increase as businesses hurried to establish an online presence. Network administrators became essential, managing the complex infrastructure that supported the expansion of the Internet.

The role of IT support specialists has become crucial for handling the technical challenges of this new era. Although the BLS did not track jobs specifically labeled as "artificial intelligence" in the 1990s, automation and data processing—key aspects of AI—were already affecting the labor market. For example, the decline in clerical and administrative support roles reflects early efficiency gains that more advanced AI-driven systems would later build on. Tasks such as data entry and managing basic customer inquiries became automated, reducing the need for large human teams in these areas of function.

Over the decade, BLS data from "Employment and Earnings" shows a shift away from manual, clerical jobs toward roles requiring more cognitive skills and technical expertise, even if they are not directly related to AI. This shift is transforming industries; for example, the rise of e-commerce has reduced the need for retail jobs such as sales clerks and cashiers as physical stores face increasing competition.

As automated customer service developed, laying the groundwork for modern AI chatbots, the need for large call center operations decreased. At the same time, manufacturing automation, already growing, accelerated with the adoption of digital technologies, resulting in fewer jobs involving repetitive manual work. Although it's difficult at this early stage to connect this trend directly to "AI," the pattern of technology reducing human tasks was evident, hinting at AI's eventual influence. (U.S. Bureau of Labor Statistics, Employment and Earnings, Reports 1990-1999)

By 1994, the Internet had become a part of everyday life, with the Mosaic web browser marking the Web's birth. Popular gadgets included Power Rangers action figures, the Apple Newton Message Pad, and the Sony PlayStation, which revolutionized gaming. Innovations like the Apple PowerBook with a color screen pushed technological boundaries. In the late 1990s, digital cameras and GPS improved memory capturing and navigation, increasing the societal impact of the Internet and AI.

The .com boom sped up these trends, making the Internet vital to daily life. Broadband connections support dynamic, interactive websites and AI-powered recommendation engines, improving e-commerce and online search. These advances changed consumer habits and business models, laying the groundwork for the digital world of the 2000s.

In the 1990s, automation mainly consisted of single-purpose machines designed for repetitive tasks in controlled environments. Today, automation has developed into a connected, intelligent system capable of managing complex, data-driven, and adaptable processes across various industries and daily life. The number of industrial robots has increased by more than 400% since the 1990s, indicating significant growth in scale and capabilities.

Fast forward, modern industrial automation uses collaborative robots, smart sensors, and machine vision, which are easier to program and integrate into existing workflows. Advances in edge computing and real-time data analysis have boosted manufacturing efficiency, allowing fewer workers to produce more output. AI and machine learning have improved automation, enabling complex decision-making in customer support, data collection, trading, and analytics. IoT has made smart home technology widespread and affordable, letting users control thermostats, lighting, security systems, and voice assistants.

Robotics and AI have driven the development of autonomous machines, such as self-driving cars and cleaning robots, which were once considered science fiction in 1990. Today, automation connects entire supply chains and operations, reaching levels of integration that were impossible in the 1990s. Overall, automation has evolved from standalone, single-purpose devices to a vast network of intelligent systems that manage complex, data-driven tasks in industry and everyday life.

The 1990s, marked by the rapid expansion of the World Wide Web, transformed how society develops technology. What began as a niche tool for academic and military purposes grew into a global phenomenon, driven by Tim Berners-Lee's revolutionary inventions and the rise of user-friendly graphical web browsers. This era experienced an unprecedented surge in users and content, fueling the dot-com boom and establishing e-commerce and online communication, such as email, as essential.

The Internet was aptly called the "information superhighway," with personal computers playing a crucial role in its development. This era marked a significant shift in how people interacted with technology, characterized by exploration, widespread connectivity, and unprecedented access to information. It transformed how people consumed news, shopped, communicated, and searched for information and entertainment.

As society became more dependent on digital infrastructure for daily needs, this reliance started to overshadow the initial optimism of the decade. Technological progress provided new opportunities but also created significant labor market challenges, as the "information superhighway" disrupted established industries and prompted a rethinking of work. According to official labor statistics from the U.S. Bureau of Labor Statistics, such as those in "Employment and Earnings," there was strong overall job growth driven by the expanding technology sector.

New roles such as web developers, network administrators, and IT support specialists emerged and grew rapidly, highlighting the urgent need for businesses to establish an online presence. However, behind this growth was a story of displacement. The rise of e-commerce has reduced the dominance of traditional brick-and-mortar stores, affecting jobs for sales clerks and cashiers. Automation, a key part of many new online platforms, has made labor-intensive processes more efficient, pointing to a future where human roles shift toward oversight and specialized problem-solving rather than manual labor.

The 1990s marked a pivotal era in human-technology history, featuring exciting advancements and disruptions. The Internet transformed employment by boosting technical roles and making some jobs obsolete. Increased reliance on digital technologies affected health, with sedentary habits contributing to obesity and other health issues, illustrating the physical effects of the "information superhighway." It sparked debates on technology's influence on work, well-being, and daily life, debates that continued and deepened in subsequent years.

9

The Digital Transformation from 2000 to 2020—Technology, Labor, and Public Health

I n the 2000s, a typical family day involved transitioning from dial-up to broadband internet, the rise of personal entertainment devices, and the merging of work, school, and home life. Additionally, concerns grew about the media's possible influence on families. Technological breakthroughs in 2000 ushered in the digital age and changed culture.

Early automation depended on specialized tools for routine tasks. A significant milestone in the digital revolution occurred in the early 2000s, bringing about rapid technological progress and cultural shifts in the U.S. It began with the burst of the dot-com bubble, which challenged many internet venture companies.

The 9/11 attacks in 2001 had a profound impact on history and prompted major policy and security reforms. The decade then concluded with a nationwide financial crisis. The 9/11 attacks were crucial in changing how we travel, communicate, and view the world. The government's determination helped revive American innovation and cultural influence. Technology continued to advance, with digital tools becoming common and social media connecting people worldwide.

The Dawn of a New Millennium

The housing market in 2000 contrasted with the rapid digital evolution. Property values soared, driven by a strong economy and low interest rates. Homeownership became a significant milestone, but the boom laid the groundwork for a bubble that quickly burst, leading to a market correction in later years.

As the millennium advanced, the cost of everyday groceries remained stable. Ground beef averaged $1.45 per pound, a slight increase from the previous year, while eggs cost about $0.92 per dozen, a modest decrease that helped families stay within their budgets. Houses sold quickly as prices rose, interest rates remained low, and buyers faced stiff competition. The average mortgage rate hovered around 8.5%, making homeownership more attainable for many. Typical suburban homes ranged from $150,000 to $200,000, and sellers often received multiple offers due to strong demand.

The early 2000s set the stage for technological progress and cultural shifts as the world moved into the digital era. Innovations in entertainment and technology influenced the future, evidenced by streaming platforms like Netflix transforming traditional media. The healthcare and renewable energy fields also demonstrated potential, marked by breakthroughs in medical research and a rising focus on sustainability.

Innovative industries and companies emerged, shaping the future. Social media platforms like Facebook (launched in 2004) and Twitter (introduced in 2006) transformed communication, social interactions, and political discourse across the United States. Technology giants such as Apple, Google, and Microsoft have become essential to daily life. Apple's iPhone, introduced in 2007, revolutionized mobile communication. Google's search engine and online services dominated the digital landscape, while Microsoft solidified its position with Windows.

As technology advanced rapidly, other sectors encountered challenges. Traditional media struggled as streaming gained popularity, while healthcare faced increasing costs and an aging population. Technological innovations appeared in toys like Furby, Pokémon cards, and video games. Home entertainment expanded with flat-screen TVs, DVD players, and popular mobile phones such as the Motorola V60 and Nokia 3310.

Entertainment thrived during this period. Faith Hill's "Breathe" topped the Billboard Hot 100, winning hearts with its emotional lyrics and country-pop blend. The sci-fi hit "Mission: Impossible II," which earned over $546 million worldwide, dominated the box office. Video games, streaming services, and Hollywood continued shaping global entertainment. The release of the Sony PlayStation 2 revolutionized home entertainment by providing immersive gaming and DVD playback.

Innovations like Bluetooth-enabled seamless device connectivity and the Rio PMP300 changed how people listened to music with portable MP3 players. The Canon EOS D30, a digital SLR camera, made high-resolution photography accessible to everyone. The Internet matured in the 2000s, fueled by the rise of social media platforms. Facebook became a leading social network, while Twitter grew into a global hub for news and real-time conversations before rebranding as X. These platforms profoundly influenced social movements, political debates, and society at large.

Email and instant messaging have become standard tools, connecting people worldwide and encouraging global interaction. Broadband replaced dial-up with faster internet access, and wireless networks allowed flexible communication. The digital revolution accelerated, making the Internet a vital part of daily life. These technologies transformed online life, changing work, communication, and entertainment. Key innovations in 2000 shaped the future.

From Gas to Electric Vehicles

The automobile industry underwent significant changes as technological progress disrupted traditional manufacturing and design. Electric vehicles (EVs) gained popularity, challenging internal combustion engines. Tesla became a leader, capturing the attention of environmentally conscious consumers with sleek designs and autonomous driving features. Traditional automakers scrambled to adapt, with some investing in EV research and development, while others faced financial difficulties and bankruptcy.

Strategic mergers and acquisitions became common as companies vied for dominance in the EV market. In-car entertainment and navigation systems were developed, with Apple CarPlay and Android Auto enabling seamless smartphone integration, blurring the lines between personal devices and vehicles. Top-selling cars reflected shifting consumer preferences: the Toyota Camry for reliability, the Honda Civic for efficiency and customization, and Tesla's Model S and Model 3 for advanced technology and distinctive driving experiences.

How Smartphones Shape Our Choices

Throughout the 2010s, the smartphone became the primary interface for daily interaction with technology. Mobile devices have become an essential part of people's lives, providing constant access to the Internet, social media, and a wide variety of applications. This ongoing connectivity fostered an environment where smartphones act as virtual extensions of their users, allowing for deep personalization and a persistent, often unconscious reliance on algorithmic systems' decision-making.

The rapid expansion of Big Data defined the past decade, as each online interaction, app use, and device communication generated vast data. Artificial intelligence, fueled by these large datasets, gradually impacted daily life via recommendation systems, targeted advertising, and predictive text. Meanwhile, the Internet of Things (IoT) grew in prominence, with smart home gadgets and wearable devices becoming more prevalent, enhancing overall connectivity.

Fading Professions, Rising Codes

The Bureau of Labor Statistics shows growth in computer and mathematical jobs, driven by the expansion of the tech sector and increasing dependence on AI. At the same time, clerical and manufacturing roles declined due to automation. IoT has opened up opportunities in hardware engineering, embedded software, and device maintenance, while slowly reducing jobs in manual diagnostics and roles for non-networked device appliances. These technological advances have significantly changed the global labor market. The rise of Big Data and AI has created new roles such as data scientists, AI ethicists, and UX designers, who play a key role in improving digital experiences. Meanwhile, automation has decreased efficiency and precision.

The Health Effects of Digital Engagement

A shift to the digital economy prompted a reevaluation of workforce development strategies. Schools and vocational training programs began emphasizing critical thinking, digital literacy, and adaptability, preparing individuals to work with and alongside advanced technologies. The main challenge became ensuring that human qualities—creativity, ethical judgment, and nuanced decision-making—remained vital in an era shaped by AI's invisible influence.

While the 2010s brought unprecedented convenience and access, they also created significant public health problems. The ease of using smartphones and IoT devices at home contributed to a quiet epidemic of decreased physical activity and sedentary lifestyles. Algorithmic recommendation engines designed to increase engagement led to longer screen time, less outdoor activity, and higher obesity rates and chronic health issues.

At least 21 state legislatures have begun reforms in K–12 media and information literacy education, including significant updates in California, Delaware, Illinois, and New Jersey (U.S. Media Literacy Policy Report, Media Literacy Now, 2024). These efforts, mostly bipartisan, seek to tackle challenges that many school curricula still overlook—such as distinguishing true from false information online, recognizing AI-generated content, and using social media safely.

The most comprehensive programs, currently being developed and tested for K–12 students, also aim to teach them how to locate and evaluate online sources and to think critically about how generative AI creates content. They also educate students about digital citizenship, which involves engaging with others online respectfully. This increasing dependence on technology—bolstered by Big Data and AI—has led to visible physical effects.

Personalized ads often promote high-calorie foods and entertainment, reinforcing unhealthy habits. The constant stimulation and instant gratification from mobile devices disrupt sleep patterns, raise stress levels, and lead to metabolic problems. Interfaces designed for extended use have contributed to poor posture and repetitive strain injuries, while the seamless integration of technology into daily life has made physical activity less necessary.

The impact of technological immersion extends beyond just acquiring technical skills, emphasizing the importance of understanding the link between technology and human physiology. As educational systems adapt to meet the needs of the digital economy, they must also address the urgent health issues caused by constant digital engagement. Relying on AI for decision-making reduces opportunities for hands-on experience and kinesthetic learning, thereby lowering physical literacy. Moving forward, the challenge will be to foster AI collaboration while safeguarding physical health and well-being, as technology becomes more integrated into every aspect of life.

The Fourth Industrial Revolution

The Fourth Industrial Revolution (4IR) signifies a distinct era characterized by the convergence of technologies that blur the lines between the physical, digital, and biological realms. It stems from the fundamental changes introduced by the previous three revolutions, each building upon the infrastructure and innovations established earlier. Essentially, the first three revolutions concentrated on mechanization, mass production, and automation.

The Fourth Industrial Revolution is about creating intelligent, interconnected ecosystems that integrate data and technology into every aspect of life and industry. Industry and technology have progressed through several key transitions, each building upon innovations from earlier periods.

The journey began with mechanization, replacing manual labor and animal power with machines, marking the start of the First Industrial Revolution. This significant change boosted productivity and laid the foundation for future progress. The next important step was automation. With automated systems, industries could perform repetitive tasks with minimal human effort. This phase introduced self-regulating technologies and coincided with the Second Industrial Revolution, transforming manufacturing and other sectors by enabling more consistent and scalable operations.

Digital control emerged as computers became essential in industrial processes. Using computers enhanced accuracy, flexibility, and data management beyond what analog systems could offer. This shift became a fundamental part of the digital revolution, enabling more advanced management and optimization of complex systems.

The expansion of Internet-connected devices worldwide, facilitating seamless communication, and the rise of the Internet of Things (IoT). Today, IoT is vital to Industry 4.0, enabling real-time monitoring and control by linking physical devices to digital platforms. Artificial intelligence (AI) has further advanced these technological capabilities.

With AI, machines can learn, make decisions, and recognize patterns, enabling intelligent automation that adapts to changing conditions in real time. This progress is transforming both industrial and software processes by enabling dynamic problem-solving and continuous improvement.

Quantum computing represents the newest frontier. Drawing on principles of quantum mechanics, this emerging technology aims to solve problems beyond the reach of classical computers. Its potential applications include breakthroughs in artificial intelligence, pharmaceuticals, and logistics, opening fresh paths for innovation and efficiency.

Together, these technologies are driving us into an era governed by interconnected and intelligent systems. AI enhances automation by making processes more adaptive and responsive. When combined with quantum computing, AI's capabilities become even more powerful, enabling rapid progress and discoveries.

The Internet remains the backbone of this transformation, enabling real-time communication between physical operations and their digital counterparts, known as digital twins. These feedback loops support ongoing optimization and improvements. The combination of mechanization, automation, digital control, the Internet, AI, and quantum computing is advancing intelligent automation. These technologies enable systems to learn and solve problems with minimal human input, accelerating progress in areas such as supply chain management, pharmaceutical research, and industrial efficiency.

The main difference among mechanization, automation, and AI lies in the types of work they replace and their ability to operate and adapt independently. Mechanization involves replacing physical tasks with machines but still depends on human oversight. Automation handles both physical and specific mental functions by following predefined rules without human intervention for processes. AI goes further by simulating human intelligence, enabling systems to learn, adapt, and make decisions in unpredictable, dynamic environments that are not explicitly programmed.

Mechanization provided us with machine power; automation delivered consistently, rule-based efficiency; and AI introduced machine cognition and adaptability. While all AI is a type of automation, not every automation has AI's ability to learn and make decisions independently.

IV

The Era of Ubiquitous Technology and AI (2020s-2050)

Part 4 offers an insightful look into a future shaped by AI and emerging technologies. Focusing on the years 2035, 2040, and 2050, it explores possible future scenarios based on current technological trends and discusses their wide-ranging potential impacts. The writing presents complex ideas about AI and automation, and their influence on sectors such as labor, education, and health, in a clear and accessible way. It raises crucial questions about the ethical, societal, and personal effects.

10

Looking to The Future (2020–2050)

I n the 2020s, a typical family day involves extensive use of technology throughout all aspects of home life, from work and school to entertainment and daily chores. This reliance increased during the COVID-19 pandemic, accelerating existing trends such as remote work, online learning, and telehealth. During this crisis, digital tools became essential for maintaining societal functions, with smartphones, high-speed internet, and cloud services shifting from conveniences to necessary parts of daily life. At this point, society has not only adapted to the extremely hot temperatures in the pot but has also become dependent on a piping-hot technology ecosystem.

Global competition, data availability, and the demand for responsible development are shaping today's AI landscape. Governments around the world are investing heavily in AI research for national security and economic growth, influencing which AI areas—such as specific algorithms and data infrastructure—receive the most focus. The debate over human factors is at the forefront, with concerns about job displacement, algorithmic bias, and the need for human oversight driving calls for regulation.

Policy discussions actively shape how AI is developed and used, stressing ethical principles and responsible deployment. Marketing promotes AI as a solution to significant issues such as health and climate, but companies also face criticism when AI appears exploitative. They focus on developing "trustworthy" AI to meet market needs and stay ahead of competitors.

Artificial intelligence is becoming more advanced, powering applications from voice assistants to complex medical diagnostics. This development has led to extensive debates about AI ethics, data privacy, and the impact of automation on employment. As digital and physical boundaries increasingly overlap, augmented reality (AR) and virtual reality (VR) technologies demonstrate significant potential.

Remote work, driven by high-speed internet and cloud technology, is becoming more common. This shift has increased the need for cybersecurity specialists, data analysts, and digital project managers. Once considered specialized, these roles are now vital for both businesses and society. Telemedicine has opened new opportunities in virtual patient care and health informatics, while advances in artificial intelligence are surpassing traditional methods jobs.

As automation reduces repetitive jobs in manufacturing, data entry, and administration, new positions that blend human skills with AI—such as AI trainers—have emerged. Roles that require creativity, critical thinking, and emotional intelligence have grown more valuable, prompting ongoing skill development and a renewed appreciation for human contributions.

Labor statistics from this period showed a growing gap between those with digital fluency and those whose skills became outdated. Reports from organizations like the International Labor Organization (ILO) and national statistical agencies emphasized both the resilience of technology and the displacement it caused. The merging of digital and physical environments, enabled by AR and VR technologies, signals the rise of jobs that will require a blend of technical skills and creativity. This period marks a significant shift in work practices and redefines individuals' roles within an interconnected ecosystem.

In 2021 and 2022, the ILO observed significant growth in digital project management, cybersecurity, and cloud infrastructure, with some sectors seeing annual job increases of over 30%. Meanwhile, the U.S. Bureau of Labor Statistics (BLS) reported a 15–20% decline in routine administrative assistant roles. Additionally, a LinkedIn workforce report noted that telemedicine created new jobs, especially in health informatics and virtual patient advocacy. In 2022, global job postings for these roles increased by more than 25%.

AI's progress has led to both job losses and gains. Jobs that depend on repetitive mental and manual work—like basic bookkeeping, content moderation, and simple data tasks—have steadily declined. The BLS estimates that automation might replace up to 10% of workers in these fields by 2030. On the other hand, new roles such as "AI Ethicists," "Prompt Engineers," and "Human-AI Collaboration Specialists" have grown significantly, indicating a shift towards enhancing human abilities rather than replacing them.

The merging of digital and physical realms, accelerated by AR and VR, suggests future jobs will require both technical and creative abilities. The World Economic Forum's "Future of Jobs Report 2023" highlights the increasing value of critical thinking, creativity, and emotional intelligence—skills that AI cannot easily imitate. This period demands ongoing skill development and a reassessment of human contributions in a hybrid workforce.

Between 2020 and 2023, the educational landscape experienced notable changes reflecting shifts in the labor market. Enrollment in online courses and digital platforms grew significantly, with the online education market projected to exceed $370 billion by 2026 (Global Market Insights, 2023).

Universities and vocational institutions expanded their remote learning options, increasing demand for educators skilled in digital pedagogy and instructional design. Additionally, specialized training programs, such as data science, cybersecurity, and AI bootcamps, have gained popularity, underscoring the need to adapt educational pathways to technological progress.

The rapid progress of AI widened the skills gap, deepening existing inequalities and exposing the limitations of traditional educational models. As AI systems became capable of performing complex tasks, the need for easily automated skills, such as basic data entry and routine problem-solving, declined. Meanwhile, higher-level skills—such as critical thinking, problem-solving, creativity, emotional intelligence, and the ability to collaborate with AI—became increasingly essential. Those lacking these advanced skills or familiarity with AI technologies faced significant challenges and disadvantages.

The World Economic Forum predicted that by 2025, a large portion of the global workforce will need to reskill or upskill (World Economic Forum, 2020). This challenge highlighted the urgent need to change educational priorities and methods to keep pace with technological progress. In response, academic institutions began incorporating AI literacy and ethics into their curricula to foster understanding rather than fear of these technologies. New degree programs and certifications for roles such as "AI trainers" and "prompt engineers" emerged. Additionally, lifelong learning initiatives became more popular, focusing on developing adaptable skills that can be used across various fields and industries.

The integration of the digital and physical worlds has enabled immersive learning experiences through AR and VR, offering more engaging, practical training for future careers. However, ensuring equitable access to these technologies remains a significant challenge, as rapid technological change risks increasing the gap between those who can adapt and those who cannot.

The increasing technological partnership has significantly affected human physical and mental health. As reliance on digital tools for work, education, and social interactions grew, sedentary lifestyles also expanded, leading to a worldwide increase in health problems and weight gain. With smartphones, high-speed internet, and cloud computing now essential parts of everyday life, opportunities for physical activity have decreased.

Remote work blurred the distinction between personal and professional time, leading to more extended sitting periods and more digital distractions that hindered physical activity. Although telemedicine improved healthcare access, it reduced the need for in-person visits, cutting down on incidental movement and social interaction. The advanced AI technology also encouraged passive consumption of digital content, further promoting sedentary behavior.

The widespread use of technology, like smartphones and personal computers, is a double-edged sword. While constant connectivity promotes resilience and innovation, it also increases screen time. This sedentary lifestyle, characterized by less physical activity and a diet of more processed, convenient foods during digital device use, is associated with rising rates of obesity, heart disease, and metabolic disorders.

Research by the World Health Organization (WHO) after 2020 shows that increased technology use is linked to decreased physical activity. The growth in online grocery shopping and targeted advertising has led to higher consumption of calorie-dense foods, raising public health concerns that need further investigation. These same technologies, created for connection and efficiency, have unintentionally contributed to this challenge.

Beyond physical health, digital immersion has affected mental well-being by fostering new dependencies. The blurred boundaries between digital and physical worlds often resulted in virtual interactions replacing face-to-face connections, increasing feelings of isolation and anxiety. Continuous streams of information guided by AI algorithms tended to reinforce echo chambers and cause mental fatigue, while dopamine hits from social media encouraged digital addiction.

Despite progress in AR and VR, which offer immersive learning and social experiences, they also carry risks of disconnecting from reality and worsening mental health issues. The well-known bond between humans and technology requires careful reevaluation, prompting urgent discussions on digital wellness and the potential long-term health impacts of this growing relationship.

Between 2020 and 2023, society saw significant changes driven by a stronger connection to technology. Digital integration boosted resilience and innovation but also transformed labor markets, education, and healthcare. This period underscored the importance of learning new skills and adapting continuously, with artificial intelligence acting as both a driver for progress and a challenge. Some educational systems adapted, but unevenly, increasing social disparities. Digital immersion affects both physical and mental health, highlighting the need for balanced use. Technology should improve human experiences, which requires intentional effort to support well-being and cohesion.

In July 2025, the White House released "Winning the Race: America's AI Action Plan," outlining the Trump administration's push for significant AI infrastructure that relies on data centers and skilled trade workers. The plan highlights labor shortages as a primary challenge, pointing out the workforce as a key constraint alongside GPUs, capital, and power. Companies like Google, Microsoft, Amazon, and TSMC are investing in training programs and partnerships to close this gap, but efforts may fall short of demand.

In 2025, the U.S. government reduced student loan eligibility for architecture and education, as they are no longer considered professional degrees. The Repayment Assistance Plan (RAP) will replace previous loan programs and limit borrowing to $20,500 per year ($100,000 total) for graduate students and $50,000 per year ($200,000 total) for professional students.

Previously, graduate students could borrow up to the full cost of their degree. The American Institute of Architects opposes reclassifying architects as non-professionals, arguing this change undermines the profession and limits access to architectural education. Students in nursing, physical therapy, dental hygiene, occupational therapy, and social work will see reduced loans, raising concerns from the American Association of Colleges of Nursing. The Trump administration proposals would cap federal nursing loans at $100,000, while fields like pharmacy, law, medicine, and dentistry could receive up to $200,000. Health care groups have voiced concerns about this change.

Advanced degrees often open doors to high-paying jobs, making it a complex decision for those planning their careers. They must weigh the benefit of avoiding debt and entering well-paid trades now against the potential for higher education to lead to better jobs and bigger salaries later. This ongoing debate continues to shape the choices and ambitions of newcomers to the job market.'

AI will be integral to everyday life by 2030. Traditional devices like keyboards, mice, and smartphones will become obsolete, replaced by voice control, gesture recognition, and AI helpers that handle routine tasks. Self-driving cars, intelligent assistants, and immersive AR displays will become common.

By 2030, cities will feature a network of autonomous vehicles and efficient public transit, changing how people travel and own cars. Shared mobility and ride-hailing services will be common. AI influences cultural trends, social norms, and relationships, blurring the lines between the physical and digital worlds through augmented reality. Global digital connectivity enables instant communication, making physical distance irrelevant.

Digital innovation transforms education, healthcare, and entertainment. Students participate in virtual classrooms and collaborate globally—healthcare benefits from remote consultations and AI-guided diagnoses, improving access. Entertainment advances into immersive virtual reality experiences that respond to users' actions and emotions.

Since the start of the digital revolution in 2000, the United States has experienced significant changes in technology, culture, and daily life. The adoption of advanced digital tools has influenced society, industries, and individual experiences, paving the way for a future of prosperity, innovation, and growth possibilities.

2035: A Society Transformed by AI

Imagine it's 2035, and the US leads the AI revolution, transforming society and markets. Algorithms replace humans in trading by analyzing data to make better decisions. This shift reduces personal connection, creating a new investor type who values AI's efficiency but also seeks human creativity and emotional intelligence.

By combining machine analysis with human intuition, these investors aim to navigate the changing market landscape. The rise of AI has impacted the American dream and the paths to success. Employment has evolved, with jobs now requiring a wider variety of skills to keep up with technological advancements.

Automation plays a vital role in everyday life, making tasks easier and providing unmatched convenience. Self-driving cars navigate busy streets, while smart homes anticipate their owners' needs, blurring the lines between the physical and digital worlds. This technological integration allows individuals to focus on their passions and entrepreneurial pursuits, as daily chores become obsolete.

Education has shifted its core principles to meet the needs of a technology-driven future. Schools and universities have adopted progressive curricula, making coding and programming as vital as reading and writing. Children as young as five learn the basics of robotics and machine learning. Classrooms combine traditional academics with advanced technology, using interactive holographic lessons and virtual field trips to promote global awareness and understanding engagement.

Society has adjusted to these changes, with AI assistants now managing schedules, making reservations, and simplifying daily tasks. The skills needed for success have become more critical, and people rely more on technology to support their routines.

American eating habits have shifted to prioritize health and sustainability. Plant-based diets and lab-grown meats are now standard, and urban areas incorporate vertical farming and hydroponic systems, redefining the idea of "farm-to-table." Living spaces have modernized, with smart homes featuring AI-powered systems that control temperature, lighting, and security through voice commands.

Mobility has undergone significant changes. Self-driving cars are now standard, and vehicle ownership has shifted to subscription models that grant access to fleets of autonomous vehicles. Commuting time has become an opportunity for work or leisure, as people rely on their cars to get to their destinations.

AI includes computer systems that mimic human intelligence, such as learning and reasoning. It has improved efficiency in areas like autonomous vehicles and smart devices. Experts highlight ethical concerns and stress the importance of human oversight to prevent misuse. As AI becomes more integrated into daily life, concerns about ethics and accountability grow more urgent. Additionally, AI holds great potential in healthcare, enabling accurate diagnoses and personalized treatments, but issues such as data privacy and algorithmic bias remain significant. Imagine that!

In finance, AI can detect fraud and improve investment strategies, but it also introduces risks, such as algorithmic bias and market manipulation. Society needs to decide whether programmers, data scientists, or deploying companies should be held accountable for AI mistakes. Setting clear guidelines and accountability is essential for maintaining trust and ensuring ethical practices standards.

Quantum computing is a groundbreaking technology that uses quantum mechanics to deliver extraordinary computational power. Although it has the potential to revolutionize areas such as cryptography and drug development, it also poses security challenges, rendering current encryption methods obsolete. AI and quantum computing provide significant advantages but also pose new difficulties. Using these technologies is essential for promoting fairness, accountability, equality, and privacy. Careful planning is needed to achieve positive results.

2040: AI Integration and Societal Change

Let's imagine it's the year 2040, and the United States continues to lead the way in the artificial intelligence revolution. This scenario offers a speculative yet plausible view of how life and technology might evolve, drawing on current trends and their potential impacts. Artificial intelligence has become an essential part of everyday life in America, transforming homes, workplaces, communities, and even the idea of creativity. By 2040, AI will enhance housing design, construction, and management. Systems will match people with homes based on their needs and income, and modular, adaptable spaces will become standard. This will elevate customization to a new level.

The entertainment industry, especially in places like Vegas, has adopted AI to improve visitor experiences. Casinos now feature holographic displays, AI-driven games, and virtual reality attractions, creating immersive environments. Ethical concerns remain about fairness, addiction, and the potential exploitation of vulnerable individuals, underscoring the need for responsible practices and governance.

AI-driven trading has become standard, with machine learning models analyzing market data in real time to guide investment strategies. A new group of investors, "AI-vectors," relies on AI to manage portfolios and execute trades. While this has driven significant progress, it also raises concerns about market manipulation and unfair advantages. Regulators are working to enhance transparency and fairness in the growing financial sector landscape.

Technology has transformed work, making remote jobs more common and reducing reliance on offices. Longer lifespans boost demand for caregivers, while environmental issues and AI advances create roles in sustainability and ethics. AI is revolutionizing creative industries and prompting questions of ownership. Brain-computer interfaces and cybernetic enhancements merge humans and machines, offering new opportunities but raising ethical concerns.

Meanwhile, some adopt digital minimalism, focusing on meaningful connections and leading simpler lives with technology. Virtual and augmented reality technologies have integrated, creating interactive entertainment that blends the digital and physical worlds. Additionally, high-speed transportation methods such as hyperloop networks and electric aircraft have transformed travel, enabling people to reach faraway destinations within a single day.

The rapid advancement of technology makes continuous learning essential. Skills and knowledge can quickly become outdated, requiring adaptation to stay relevant. Progress in nanotechnology and biology has transformed healthcare, allowing for precise, personalized treatments. Diseases like cancer and genetic disorders are now more manageable, with a focus on prediction and prevention. However, these innovations also raise privacy and data security issues, highlighting the importance of cybersecurity professionals in protecting personal information systems.

American lifestyles now prioritize personalization, wellness, and environmental responsibility, with smart homes and wearable devices managing daily routines and health. Online communities and virtual reality platforms offer new ways to connect, while concerns about mental health and the environment have sparked a renewed interest in nature.

Automation and artificial intelligence play a crucial role in everyday life, with well-known examples like self-driving cars and smart homes. Virtual and augmented reality have revolutionized entertainment and education by offering engaging, immersive experiences. Furthermore, data analytics and AI deliver personalized recommendations for various needs, such as organizing daily routines and managing health and wellness.

Education systems now use blended learning models that combine online and in-person teaching. Virtual classrooms link students worldwide, encouraging collaboration and cultural exchange. Additionally, holographic lessons and simulations enhance learning by making academic subjects more engaging.

2050: The New Age of Everyday Life

The year is 2050, and the United States leads the AI revolution. Artificial intelligence now plays a central role in daily life across America, transforming homes, workplaces, communities, and even the idea of creativity itself. Since the early 2000s, the U.S. has made significant technological progress. By 2050, AI is expected to manage everyday household tasks like climate control and cooking. In public spaces, AI will optimize traffic with autonomous vehicles and oversee energy use.

The workplace will have changed significantly by 2050, with automation replacing many traditional jobs. Human roles will shift toward supervision, ethics, and AI project development. The partnership between humans and machines in creative fields shows how generative AI supports artists, musicians, and writers in creating innovative works and exploring new storytelling methods and paths.

This period marks a societal shift in valuing creativity and human ingenuity. The role of AI in art sparks debate, prompting a reevaluation of genuine artistic work. Educational institutions now focus on skills such as AI interaction, data analysis, and critical thinking to prepare for a future in which human insight guides machines. While AI eases daily tasks, it raises ethical concerns, emphasizing the need for regulations on data privacy, algorithm accountability, and equitable access to technology.

Looking ahead to 2050, the ongoing pursuit of seamless efficiency through Artificial Intelligence will probably embed technology into all aspects of daily life, turning routine activities into managed experiences. While this development offers considerable advantages, it may also entail latent costs that society should proactively identify and address.

AI will have achieved humanity's goal of deep, predictive integration into daily life. The system emphasizes comfort and efficiency but demands a new level of social and personal responsibility. Your AI assistant Aura quietly wakes you by adjusting your surroundings using biometric data and predictive analytics, replacing the traditional alarm.

Scenario: A Tuesday Morning in Atlanta, 2050

At 6:30 AM, Aura begins the wake-up process. The bright glass windows in the bedroom slowly transition from opaque to transparent, perfectly aligned with sunrise simulations tailored to your optimized sleep cycle data from the previous night's continuous health monitoring.

Good morning, Alex," Aura whispers in a synthesized voice designed to reduce cortisol levels. "Your sleep efficiency score was 94%—optimal. Your autonomous vehicle, Unit 734, is two minutes away from the curb and scheduled for a 7:15 AM departure."

As you brush your teeth, Aura informs you: "Your personalized schedule today features the 9 AM client call you asked to move earlier, given the weather pattern I forecasted yesterday. Traffic data indicates a six-minute shorter commute today. Would you prefer a high-protein smoothie or your usual optimized nutrient coffee blend?"

The benefits are clear: a life free from traffic stress, optimized for health, and perfectly scheduled for productivity. Yet, this seamless existence comes with steep hidden costs and requires constant management.

Alex woke at 6:30 AM because Aura, the AI, had chosen that time. The system overrides personal decisions in favor of predicted 'optimal' outcomes, handling traffic, daily plans, and meals.

When the system fails or if Alex chooses not to use innovative features, basic life skills can deteriorate. Who is responsible if Aura makes a mistake? If the AI causes a traffic jam or miscalculates nutrients, it's unclear—who is liable? Is it the user for trusting the system, the manufacturer, or the developer?

By 2050, society will need to actively manage these trade-offs. Successfully leveraging AI's benefits while reducing its risks demands proactive decisions rather than passive acceptance. Education should focus on cultivating critical thinking rather than convenience, enabling citizens to function independently of optimized systems and to identify when to challenge algorithmic outputs.

Legal systems will need to clearly assign liability for AI, making individuals and corporations accountable for the technology they create and use. This approach underscores collective responsibility for shaping technological progress.

The Invisible Infrastructure

Amazon Web Services (AWS) is a comprehensive, widely adopted cloud computing platform that provides on-demand IT resources over the internet using a pay-as-you-go pricing model. AWS offers a broad range of services, including computing power, storage, and databases, enabling organizations to lower operational costs and scale applications with minimal upfront investment in physical hardware. With AWS, users can build, manage, and deploy applications, process large amounts of data, and deliver services from a global network of data centers.

AWS operates through a vast global network of secure data centers. Amazon manages physical hardware, security, and maintenance, while customers configure and manage the services needed to build, deploy, and grow their applications. For example, a streaming service like Netflix integrates multiple AWS services to deliver content to millions of people worldwide.

The AWS model enables organizations to sidestep the need to buy and maintain physical hardware by renting resources as needed. This pay-as-you-go approach improves cost efficiency and flexibility. For example, if a game gains more players, the company can rapidly increase computing resources via AWS, like adding blocks to expand a toy castle. This flexibility allows businesses to pay only for what they use and serve their customers more effectively.

AWS's global data center network enables applications to run closer to users, resulting in faster, more responsive digital experiences. This extensive coverage provides a key benefit, allowing businesses to reach customers worldwide without building physical infrastructure in every location. Moving from owning physical assets to using on-demand cloud resources represents a significant shift, fostering innovation and enhancing operational flexibility across various industries.

AWS's extensive network of data centers marks a major step forward in enterprise technology engagement. These centers are more than just simple server storage; they are complex ecosystems designed for performance, security, and global access. Each facility houses high-performance computer instances, large storage arrays, and advanced networking equipment. The strategic geographic placement of these centers ensures fast, reliable service and reduces latency, allowing organizations to deploy applications closer to users for a smoother experience.

As digital transformation accelerates, the demand for robust, scalable infrastructure drives rapid data center expansion. The rising adoption of IoT, artificial intelligence, machine learning, and secure storage solutions fuels the expansion. Currently, data centers are essential to society's growing digital footprint. Developing and managing these centers is a significant focus of technological progress and investment. Organizations aim to build more facilities while emphasizing energy efficiency and sustainability to lessen environmental impacts.

Placing positioning centers near reliable power and robust network sources underscores their significance. This change signifies a trend towards a distributed IT infrastructure that prioritizes accessibility and performance over server location. As the digital landscape expands, it accelerates the digital era—fueled by collaboration between AWS and Cloudflare.

Data center growth relies on service orchestrators like Cloudflare. While AWS provides the core infrastructure, Cloudflare enhances security, manages traffic, and accelerates content delivery by deploying edge servers close to users. These servers help reduce threats, localize data caching, ease the load on AWS, and boost overall performance.

Cloudflare and other service orchestrators are part of the global expansion of data centers. While AWS provides the core IT infrastructure, Cloudflare manages traffic, improves security, and accelerates content delivery from AWS data centers to users worldwide. Its edge server network, located closer to users than AWS's central regions, blocks harmful traffic and caches frequently accessed data, reducing load on AWS systems and improving responsiveness.

This synergistic relationship is vital to modern internet architecture: AWS offers power and scalability, while Cloudflare ensures accessibility, security, and performance. Without AWS infrastructure, Cloudflare would lack the services needed for protection; conversely, without Cloudflare's optimizations, AWS-hosted applications might face performance and security problems. This partnership is why your favorite streaming service rarely buffers and why online shopping feels like an effortless, instant experience built on an invisible, worldwide infrastructure. Together, they form a system that enables the smooth transfer of information and services across the digital landscape.

Today, AI-powered networks connect communities across America, making information sharing easier and supporting policy decisions. As artificial intelligence advances, it presents new opportunities and ongoing challenges for society. The ongoing shortage of skilled technicians hampers economic stability and national objectives. Although the industry increases wages, the fundamental problem remains the lack of education and training opportunities.

While the increasing number of Gen Z students choosing vocational training can help fill skills shortages, aligning social values and compensation for these roles remains challenging. Educators, industry stakeholders, and policymakers must work together to reshape educational priorities and promote skilled trades to support the country's industrial resilience and security.

The Hidden Costs of Our Tech Dependency

Growing reliance on technology, especially for communication, has transformed human interactions. It offers convenience but also diminishes in-person skills, empathy, and increases misunderstandings, social challenges, and isolation.

A key issue is the loss of subtle social cues in digital communication. They often lose the ability to interpret body language and vocal tone, crucial for meaningful face-to-face interactions. Consequently, online exchanges remain superficial, lacking the depth of traditional relationships. Technology has reduced people's capacity for genuine empathy.

When interactions happen via screens rather than in person, recognizing and understanding others' emotions becomes more difficult. Misunderstandings during direct human contact can harm relationships, as people often lack the skills needed to build deep, meaningful connections. Instant messaging enables quick communication, but can hide underlying disconnections between people.

The lack of non-verbal cues often leads to misunderstandings, causing confusion and increasing feelings of social isolation. Therefore, even with constant technological connectivity, the sense of closeness and meaningful interaction might weaken. The growing dependence on digital communication often masks deeper disconnects among individuals.

While technology can maintain ongoing contact, the absence of nonverbal cues can lead to misinterpretations. Ironically, this continuous digital interaction might result in greater social isolation, as its convenience can weaken genuine, meaningful relationships.

If the worldwide network of data centers faced a significant shortage, the impact would go well beyond the tech industry. Companies that depend on AWS's scalability and reach would experience application failures, data inaccessibility, and compromised customer service. The unseen toy box would run out, leading to a decline in innovation and service quality.

Organizations relying on a pay-as-you-go model may have to fall back on costly, inefficient physical infrastructure, risking financial strain and possible operational shutdowns. Start-ups that depend on cloud flexibility might experience growth delays. In the event of an internet outage, markets could fragment, trade could stall, and online activity could slow.

This scenario would not only disrupt businesses but also threaten society's critical infrastructure. Financial transactions, healthcare services, communication systems, and emergency response—all dependent on cloud infrastructure—could experience unprecedented outages. The flexibility and innovation driven by cloud computing would slow down, highlighting the crucial role of data centers in the digital economy and modern society.

Delta Airlines faced disruptions when AWS data center outages affected its critical systems, causing failures in booking, flight management, and customer service, resulting in worldwide passenger delays and poor experiences.

In this setting, cybersecurity proved essential. CloudStrike, a leading cyber-security company, teamed up with Delta Airlines to detect threats, respond to incidents, and protect operational systems from attacks, capitalizing on the confusion. However, the fundamental problem—the shortage of IT resources—remained, showing that even the most sophisticated security solutions cannot substitute for basic infrastructure.

The network outages caused unpredictable disruptions, including unreliable flight schedules, inaccessible passenger data, and delayed communication between ground control and aircraft. This situation highlighted the global economy's reliance on robust, distributed data centers and demonstrated that security measures alone cannot address fundamental infrastructure gaps.

The ripple effects of these disruptions reached well beyond the airline sector. Companies that depend on cloud computing face major operational issues. Financial firms struggled to process transactions, e-commerce sites experienced outages, and streaming services experienced disruptions. Key communication tools used for remote work and collaboration also became unreliable.

Hospitals and clinics were unable to retrieve patient records or provide timely care, which affected the healthcare industry. Emergency response teams struggled to coordinate aid, and educational institutions had to halt online classes. A shortage of data centers risks disrupting businesses and services that rely on cloud access and scalability.

Data centers are essential to the digital economy. Companies like AWS, Cloudflare, and CloudStrike collaborate through a global network that supports today's connected world. The challenges faced by organizations like Delta Airlines, along with wider economic and societal impacts, highlight the systemic vulnerabilities caused by data center shortages. We must invest in, innovate for, and strengthen the data center ecosystem because our digital future depends on the physical infrastructure of computation and connectivity.

By 2050, the transportation industry will look very different from its early-21st-century form. Manual driving will be rare, with personal and commercial travel mainly done by autonomous vehicles integrated into AI-controlled transit networks. Public transportation will include on-demand autonomous pods and high-speed trains, coordinated by central AI systems to maximize efficiency.

Single-purpose computing devices and paper records are now obsolete, replaced by widespread, context-aware AI interfaces and blockchain-verified digital archives. Personal AI assistants handle tasks such as managing schedules, controlling energy use, curating news feeds, and supporting creative projects, making both administrative and innovative efforts more straightforward.

The real estate industry utilizes AI for instant property valuations, predictive city planning, and autonomous building processes. Customized home designs are standard, and AI-managed fractional-ownership models are widespread. Automated, secure systems have replaced manual paper transactions and valuations.

In business and finance, automation is commonplace. AI handles supply chain management, market analysis, customer service, and financial tasks. Blockchain technology substitutes manual data entry and cash transactions, while regulations ensure privacy and economic stability.

The legal field relies on AI for tasks such as document review, predictive analytics, and digital filing. Legal experts emphasize the ethical management of AI-generated arguments and the creation of innovative strategies. AI in the penal system assists with resource allocation, rehabilitation, education, and automating manual tasks.

AI-driven diagnostic tools, personalized treatment plans, and comprehensive health monitoring systems have transformed healthcare. Secure digital archives managed by AI have superseded traditional paper records and disposable devices. Doctors now review diagnostics generated by artificial intelligence, focusing on compassionate patient care and making ethical choices.

Adaptive AI learning platforms, personalized content, and real-time feed-back systems are shaping education. Traditional textbooks, manual grading, and paper-based assignments are becoming less common, as educators promote critical thinking and creativity in AI-enhanced environments.

Entertainment and leisure have transformed through AI-curated ex-periences and immersive virtual reality. Devices designed for specific functions and traditional paper media are now seen as collectibles, while generative AI creates new forms of music, art, and storytelling. The ongoing debate about originality and human creativity remains at the forefront, with educational institutions actively encouraging critical thinking and discernment of innovation.

AI-guided robotics, drones, and integrated ecosystem management plat-forms are transforming farming practices. AI automates manual tasks, while advanced AI systems manage vertical farms and lab-grown food production facilities. These innovations enhance food security, reduce waste and environmental impact, and optimize production in line with real-time demand and nutritional needs.

Despite widespread AI adoption, the human element remains vital in areas like art and design. Human artists shape emotional and creative ideas, guiding generative AI to improve results and add meaning. Educational programs emphasize AI literacy, ethical reasoning, and originality, preparing individuals to amplify human potential by working with intelligent systems and machines.

We must prepare to address the challenges of human-machine interactions. Lifelong learning, strong regulatory frameworks, and a commitment to ethical AI use are essential for maximizing benefits and overcoming obstacles. By emphasizing human-centric skills and continuous adaptation, society can ensure that AI enhances human abilities, fostering fair development and a more enriched human experience.

The profound and multifaceted impact of the AI revolution defines the American experience in 2050. As artificial intelligence continues to advance, it affects every aspect of life, work, and creativity, bringing both new opportunities and ongoing challenges. By promoting adaptability, ethical awareness, and collaboration between humans and machines, America approaches this rapidly changing era with resilience and innovation, paving the way for a future of intentional progress.

The Boiling Frog Effect in Our Digital Lives

The boiling frog analogy illustrates how humanity's connection with technology and artificial intelligence is evolving. As digital assistants, social media, and algorithms become integral to daily life, their gradual integration resembles the story's slow rise in temperature. Each new advancement's benefits often appear to outweigh potential risks, prompting widespread acceptance. However, the genuine concern lies in the subtle, gradual erosion of autonomy and critical thinking as reliance on these technologies deepens.

As predictive algorithms become more common, machines perform tasks that need judgment, leading to small shifts and a gradual reduction in responsibility. As people adapt, their awareness of risk lessens. This slow change makes it harder to spot and respond to new threats, like a frog ignoring danger as it rises nearby.

As AI takes on more complex roles in society, the boiling-frog effect becomes clearer. Humans rely on systems with often unclear inner workings for critical decisions—from driving to healthcare diagnostics. The initial promise of greater efficiency and capabilities has led to almost total dependence, with society largely unaware of the gradual loss of control. As the distance between human oversight and machine independence narrows, we risk losing the chance to regain autonomy unless we address even small power increases.

The boiling-frog effect has seeped into daily life, especially in the realm of artificial intelligence. What started as a quest for convenience has become a hidden reliance. With each new AI integration, the heat rises, dulling awareness of the risks of losing autonomy. The greatest tragedy is failing to recognize these emerging risks until it's too late to act. The metaphor underscores the dangers of unchecked adaptation. It encourages us to think about the effects of slow change. We should stay alert and in control in a constantly changing world.

Major technological shifts display a dual dynamic: society influences technology, which then reshapes both society and individual responsibility. External regulations address systemic issues such as car safety and algorithmic bias, but with widespread modern technology, especially in communication tools, individuals must personally manage their exposure to engagement. This personal accountability is crucial because constant exposure to screens, notifications, and endless streams of content can harm mental health, productivity, and social connections' well-being.

Technology's development is shaped not by a single group but by ongoing clashes among supporters, opponents, and alternative cultures that passionately debate and oppose change. The growth of AI brings ethical debates that divide the tech industry, governments, and the public. These internal ethical discussions and external pressures are now affecting legal responsibilities and public trust in emerging technologies.

To prevent excessive technology use, people can adopt strategies that promote intentional use, set digital boundaries, and foster real-world interactions. These methods address the human motivations behind overuse—such as the need for connection, entertainment, and productivity—by directing them toward healthier activity outlets.

These include personal behavioral adjustments, educational reforms, ethical standards, and policy changes. For example, promoting digital literacy and mindful consumption helps individuals understand the pervasive presence of technology and develop intentional habits to prevent overuse. Incorporating comprehensive digital citizenship education into schools is vital; it helps students recognize the psychological effects of constant connectivity, algorithmic influence, and data privacy from an early stage.

Another practical approach is practicing mindful consumption, making conscious choices about when and why to use technology. Methods such as digital detoxes, establishing tech-free zones (like bedrooms or dining areas), and using app controls to limit screen time are beneficial.

For instance, someone might decide to replace their primary reading device, which is currently a phone or e-reader, with physical paper books. This small change creates a concrete obstacle to distraction—it's more challenging to open a physical book and check email instantly than it is on a multi-use device. Engaging physically with an offline hobby often leads to improved understanding and a more relaxed leisure experience.

Additionally, encouraging deep work and focus by scheduling dedicated periods for activities such as reading, problem-solving, or face-to-face interactions, free from digital distractions, can counteract the culture of notifications and multitasking. Maintaining offline personal interactions remains essential, balancing online connections with in-person engagement to foster social well-being.

Role modeling is also important; parents and community leaders can set positive examples by reducing recreational screen time during social gatherings, demonstrating that meaningful interactions happen in person, offline. Additionally, supporting physical community spaces like centers, libraries, parks, and other non-digital environments encourages spontaneous, human-centered interactions.

Finally, promoting ethical and human-centered technology development is crucial. We should advocate for ethical design principles, greater transparency, and regulations that clarify how algorithms influence decisions, aiding users in making informed choices. Supporting research and initiatives—like the Center for Humane Technology—encourages public dialogue and promotes responsible industry practices.

AI development should prioritize human values, ensuring that technology benefits people instead of just generating profits. Although technology displaces some jobs, it also creates new ones that often require different, more complex skills. The key issue isn't merely job loss but a significant skills mismatch.

References

Abbate, J. (1999). Inventing the Internet. MIT Press.

Abel, E. L. (2013). *The History of the Drunkometer*. Journal of Studies on Alcohol and Drugs, 74(5), 734-739.

Abish, B., & Small, G. W. (2020). Brain health consequences of digital technology use. Current Opinion in Behavioral Sciences, 36, 111-118.

AT&T. (n.d.). The history of AT&T [Historical company archives]. (Network expansion records). AT&T Corporate Archives, Location variable.

Automatic Totalisators Ltd. (n.d.). Development of the automatic totalizator [Industry historical records and patents]. (Specific patents and records document evolution)—location variable.

Berners-Lee, T. (1989). Information management: A proposal (CERN-DD-89-001-OC). CERN.

Burgee, Richard R. "A Study of Chemical Tests for Alcoholic Intoxication." Maryland Law Review, 1957, 17: 193. (Reviews chemical tests, including the Drunkometer).

Casio. (1989). Casio DA-2 [Product release].

Centers for Disease Control and Prevention (CDC). (2024, September 24). Obesity and severe obesity prevalence in adults: United States, August 2021–August 2023 (NCHS Data Brief No. 508).

Centers for Disease Control and Prevention (CDC). (n.d.). Adult obesity facts. US Department of Health and Human Services. Retrieved December 7, 2025, from https://www.cdc.gov/obesity/adult-obesity-facts/index.html

Ceruzzi, P. E. (2003). A history of modern computing (2nd ed.). The MIT Press.

Computer History Museum. (n.d.). A brief history of personal computers.

Retrieved December 7, 2025, from www.computerhistory.org

Davis, R. C. (2003). The electric starter and the democratization of the automobile. Technology and Culture, 44(2), 265–287.

Davis, R., Shrobe, H., & Szolovits, P. (1993). Common knowledge: Rethinking expert systems. MIT Press.

Department of Transportation. (2048). Autonomous Vehicle Deployment and Traffic Management Systems.

Dungan, R. (2025, November 18). Ford cannot fill high-paying, technical roles due to the US skills crisis, CEO says. HR Grapevine. https://www.hrgr apevine.com/us/content/article/2025-11-18-ford-ceo-farley-says-us-workf orce-is-held-back-by-lack-of-training

Fisher, D. E., & Slywka, B. (1990). Testimony: French scientists invent the breathalyzer [Testimony before the National Highway Traffic Safety Administration].

Ford Motor Company. (n.d.). Ford ASSET program: Technician career training. Retrieved December 7, 2025, from corporate.ford.com

Gertner, J. (2012). The idea factory: Bell Labs and the great age of American innovation. Penguin Press.

Haghjoo, P., Siri, G., Soleimani, E., Farhangi, M. A., & Alesaeidi, S. (2022). Screen time increases overweight and obesity risk among adolescents: A systematic review and dose-response meta-analysis. BMC Primary Care, 23(1), 161.

Hales, C. M., Carroll, M. D., Fryar, C. D., & Ogden, C. L. (2017). Prevalence of obesity among adults and youth: United States, 2015–2016 (NCHS Data Brief No. 288).

Harger, R. N. "An apparatus for the determination of the alcohol content of the breath." Journal of Laboratory and Clinical Medicine, 1931, 16: 306. (This is likely the foundational publication, though the specific page number is extrapolated from similar citations in the search results.)

Harger, R. N. Journal of the American Medical Association, 1940, 114: 1687. (Further work on the topic).

Harger, R. N. Science, 1931, 73: 10. (An early mention of the device in the journal Science).

Harger, R. N., E. B. Lamb, and H. R. Hulpieu. "A rapid chemical test for intoxication employing breath." Journal of the American Medical Association (JAMA), 1938, 110: 779-784. (This is a heavily cited paper, often referenced in subsequent legal and scientific discussions.)

Hollis, J. (2005). The radio hour: Radio's impact during the Great Depression. University of Michigan Press. https://fred.stlouisfed.org/series/CIVPART

Inbar, E. (2025, December 2). Ford CEO warns of 5,000 empty mechanic jobs due to skills gap [LinkedIn post]. LinkedIn. https://www.linkedin.com/posts/eladinbar_fords-ceo-jim-farley-just-revealed-america-activity-74016 66544919085057-PRAG

Institute for Advanced Technology Ethics. (2049). AI Integration and Societal Adaptation.

Internet Society. (n.d.). The birth of the Internet. Retrieved December 7, 2025, from https://www.internetsociety.org/

Isaacson, W. (2014). The innovators: How a group of hackers, geniuses, and geeks created the digital revolution. Simon & Schuster

Jones, A. W. "Measuring alcohol in blood and breath for forensic purposes – a historical review." Forensic Science Review, 2000. (A modern historical overview that references Harger's work).

L. (1923). Early mentions of artificial intelligence [Unpublished manuscript]. (Details unavailable due to historical variability).

Later articles also mention the Drunkometer in a historical and critical context:

Lecuyer, C. (2005). Machines that think: A history of personal computers. MIT Press.

Levy, A. (2025, September 23). Ford's CEO: America is ignoring the 'essential economy' as AI eats entry-level jobs—and he's building a playbook to fix it. Fortune. https://fortune.com/2025/09/23/ford-ceo-jim-farley-ai-e ating-entry-level-jobs-essential-economy/

Loeffler, G., & Craig, C. (2013). Methoxetamine misuse and toxicity. *Journal of Studies on Alcohol and Drugs, 74*(5), 816–817. https://doi.org/10.15288/jsa d.2013.74.816

Mirghani, H., & Almutairi, S. (2025, March 7). Demystifying the new dilemma of brain rot in the digital era. Cureus.

Morgan, G. A. (1923). Traffic signal (US Patent No. 1,475,074). US Patent and Trademark Office.

Mousa, T. H. (2025, July 10). Associations between screen time use and health outcomes among teenagers: United States, July 2021–December 2023. Preventing Chronic Disease, 22.

National Bureau of Economic Research (NBER). (n.d.). Historical unemployment data, 1900-present [Data set]. (Estimates compiled in various reports).

National Science Foundation. (2048). The Future of Work and Automation: 2050 Outlook.

Nintendo. (1985). Nintendo Entertainment System [Product release].

Pew Research Center. (n.d.). The digital divide: Understanding the gap. (Publication details for specific report/article not provided in search results).

Potts, W. (1920). Early traffic signal automation [Historical accounts of urban planning and technology]. (First four-way, three-color electric signal in Detroit). Location variable

Riordan, J. (2004). The origins of the Internet: A cartographic study. The Journal of Economic Perspectives, 18(2), 189–209.

Russell, S. J., & Norvig, P. (2020). Artificial intelligence: A modern approach (4th ed.). Pearson.

Scullin, M. K., & Benge, J. F. (2025, April 14). A meta-analysis of technology use and cognitive aging. Nature Human Behaviour.

Securities and Exchange Commission. (n.d.). The .com bubble and beyond. (Publication details for specific article/page not provided in search results).

Simon, H. A. (1996). The sciences of the artificial (3rd ed.). MIT Press.

Social Security Administration (SSA). (n.d.). Historical labor force participation data [Archival data and reports]. (Various historical accounts provide early 20th-century estimates.)

Stigler, G. J. (n.d.). The growth of obesity and technological change [Archival data and reports]. National Bureau of Economic Research (NBER).

Tamboer, L. M., van der Velden, R. M. J., & Verkuyten, M. (2023). Screen media overuse and associated physical, cognitive, and emotional/behavioral outcomes in children and adolescents: An integrative literature review. Child Care in Practice, 29(2), 168-191.

The History of the Internet. Internet Society. (2019, December 15). A brief history of the Internet. Retrieved December 7, 2025, from https://www.inte rnetsociety.org/internet/history-internet/brief-history-internet/

US Bureau of Labor Statistics (BLS). (n.d.). Employment situation summary [Data set and reports]. US Department of Labor. Retrieved December 7, 2025, from https://www.bls.gov/news.release/empsit.nr0.htm

US Bureau of Labor Statistics. (n.d.). Labor force participation rate [Data set]. FRED, Federal Reserve Bank of St. Louis. Retrieved December 7, 2025, from fred.stlouisfed.org

Wikipedia contributors. (n.d.). History of personal computers. Wikipedia, The Free Encyclopedia. Retrieved December 7, 2025, from https://en.wikipe dia.org/wiki/History_of_personal_computers

About the Author

Dr. Paul is a trusted business and technology consultant for the world's top investment banks, private equity firms, Fortune 100 companies, real estate firms, and business schools. He develops adaptive learning programs and helps businesses grow by leveraging AI. He's partnered with The Second City to create improv workshops and has written keynote speeches for some of TED Talks' most prominent speakers. He also has extensive experience in quantum computing, augmented intelligence, training, teaching, coaching, and leadership development.

Dr. Paul specializes in the rapid development of end-to-end eLearning, leadership programs, and Skill Labs. He is a skilled cyberpsychologist and methodologist. He leverages his knowledge and experience, as well as Artificial Intelligence. Dr. Paul is a member of several associations. He is known for being passionate, reliable, and a producer of quality. As an advocate for entrepreneurs and real estate investors, he's always had an intrinsic motivation to help others achieve their goals.

www.ingramcontent.com/pod-product-compliance
Lightning Source LLC
Chambersburg PA
CBHW020741130626
46554CB00006B/2098